# teentalk

## become a teen *with* passion and purpose!

### Sharon Witt

First published 2007 by Collective Wisdom Publications.
This edition published 2011 by Authentic Media Ltd,
52 Presley Way, Crownhill Milton Keynes, MK8 0ES.

www.authenticmedia.co.uk

17 16 15 14 13 12 11   7 6 5 4 3 2 1

**British Library Cataloguing-in-Publication Data**
A catalogue record for this book is available from the British Library.

ISBN 978-1-86024-813-9

Original typesetting and design by Communique Graphics.
This edition Temple Design. Illustrations by Karl Welsh
Printed and bound in Great Britain by Thomson Litho, Glasgow.

# grateful

## acknowledgements . . .

This book is the result of a ten-year dream that really only had wings a short time ago. Many people contributed to making this dream a reality, so I'd like to mention a few here.

Firstly, to my amazing and wonderfully supportive family: my gorgeous husband Andrew, and my two beautiful treasures, Josh and Emily. Thanks so much for supporting me in so many ways and allowing me to turn this dream into a reality. Thanks also to my friends, family members and my colleagues at MECS. To my mum and dad — thank you for supporting me in so many ways and for teaching me to be all that I am.

I must thank my amazing students — both past and present — who have encouraged me to produce a book for teens, have given helpful advice along the way, proof-read pages of my manuscript and given suggestions. Special thanks to Taylor Dykstra for coming up with the title for the **'Teen Talk'** series. To my wonderful class of Year 7 students — you have been incredibly supportive and wonderful to work with. Thank you for supporting me through a very busy time and for constantly reminding me why it is that I love working with teenagers so much. What a blessing you have been to me!

To the amazingly talented Karl Welsh — my former student and brilliant artist — thank you for saying 'yes' and creating the fantastic cartoons.

To my multi-talented editor, Paul Gallagher — thanks for your amazing support, guidance and constant encouragement. Your belief in my dream to publish this first book has meant so much to me and I thank you for the many hours you spent editing my manuscript.

Thank you Dale Beaumont — a great mentor of mine who leads by example and is truly generous in guiding others through the rigours of self-publishing. Thanks for all your support and for replying to my many emails and for saying 'yes' when I first asked to meet with you.

Thanks to Ivan and Michelle Smith at Communique Graphics for all your amazing help and guidance in producing the first book in the **'Teen Talk'** series. I am so grateful for all your help and expertise.

Finally, to the many teenagers who encouraged me to commit my thoughts to paper and who continue to inspire me daily, I hope this book inspires you. **Be everything you dream to be!**

## Enjoy!

In loving memory of

Kay Vandersluys

# What the?

## . . . there's a reason behind this book . . .

Being a teenager is, without doubt, one of the toughest things ever! When you are right in the thick of it, life can be so confusing. I have titled this book *Teen Talk* because I think we always need advice and help from people who have gone before us.

If you have picked up this book, chances are you are a young person about to enter this very tricky stage of your life. Maybe you are right in the thick of it, and perhaps need a little guidance. This book is for you, written as a guide to navigating you through to the other side of your teenage journey.

No one ever said being a teenager was easy! For some people, it can be a relatively straightforward transition in life. For others, it can be an absolute minefield of emotions, physical changes, confusion, and a whole new set of responsibilities. You were just a kid such a short time ago!

*Teen Talk* is more than a survival tool. I want you to thrive.

We'll talk about the power of goal setting, believing in your dreams, and how mistakes are not the end of the world (rather an opportunity to do better). Most importantly, I'm going to talk about how you WILL come out the other side of your teenage years knowing exactly where you want to go.

Some sections won't necessarily be relevant, whilst others may be just what you need! It is my hope that you will find many parts useful, and perhaps you can use it as a reference when you need a question answered or you are facing a particular challenge.

Wherever you are currently at, just remember that being a teenager is a stage of your life. It will end, one day! Remember that you are in control of how you get to the other side of it all. You can choose to let it be a horrendous few years, or you can embrace it! Sure, you'll be challenged along the way, but don't wish this time away. You will only ever be a teenager once, so enjoy it!

*Sharon Witt*

# foreword

**Growing up I hated reading!** I had dyslexia. Most people have heard about it, but if you haven't, it's a condition that makes words jump around a page and things really difficult to read.

So my mum sent me to tutoring every week. It helped a bit but try as I may, reading was still a challenge. I can even remember one day in Year 7 having to read the morning prayer over the school's loud speaker system. It was on a rotational basis for all the Year 7s and unfortunately my number came up.

On that particular day I missed my normal train, so I took the next one and had to run to school from the station. I just made the bell and was totally puffed. I darted straight into the school office to be met by my year co-ordinator who handed me the microphone and said, 'Okay Dale, read this passage.'

I was still recovering and with the thought that 400 other students were about to hear me read, my heart was seriously ready to pop out of my chest.

So I nervously took hold of the microphone. My knees turned to jelly, the inside of my mouth became like sandpaper and at that moment I seriously wanted to die.

For the next 45 seconds I kind of blacked-out and can't remember much. However, I do know that the prayer that I read was nothing like the prayer on the page. I was so nervous I couldn't read the words, so I pretty much mixed a bunch of sentences together and then made up the rest of it completely!

Thankfully most of the kids didn't know the prayer and most were probably half asleep still anyway, but for the rest of the day I got some really interesting looks from all the teachers.

Why am I telling you all this? **Well it's important you know things do get better!**

Fast-forward the tape, I am now 25 years old and guess what? Today I am a professional speaker and author. So far I have presented seminars to 60,000 young people in five different countries and published 16 different books.

So believe me, whatever your challenges and so-called limits are, you can do anything that you set your mind to. You just need to rise above the past (and the present for that matter) and look towards a more positive future!

I have known the author of this book, **Sharon Witt**, for quite some time. I have found her to be an exceptional human being and someone that really knows the issues young people face.

This book is a delightful read. I encourage you to soak up every word. If you are a fast reader you will breeze right through it. But if you are a slow reader (like I am still) then make sure you persist and read right to the end, because you are not only going to learn how to become truly successful in life, but you'll discover how to make the journey a lot smoother and heaps more fun!

So get reading and remember to always dream big!

*Dale Beaumont*

*International Speaker,
Bestselling Author,
Young Entrepreneur*

To find out more about Dale's books and seminars visit:
www.DaleBeaumont.com

3

# one

# Love and respect yourself

**You don't have to try**

**and be anybody else**

**but yourself . . .**

# you are unique . . .

## . . . that's a good thing

There were two versions of me at one stage when I was growing up, all because of a TV show I adored.

The show — a soap called *A Country Practice* — was very popular. Leading the way was one of the stars, 'Molly'. She was a confident, gorgeous woman who stood up for what she believed in. She dressed in bright colours and wore amazing, wacky, bright outfits.

Molly, the character, eventually died. That episode was watched by millions of Australians, sitting glued to their TVs to watch a most-loved character fade from our screens for eternity.

In front of one telly screen was me, tears rolling down, thinking how much I wanted to be 'Molly'.

The truth is, there is only one *you* on the whole face of the earth — how incredible is that!? Being created as a unique and amazing individual actually lets you off the hook straight away. You don't have to try and be anybody else but yourself. Actress Judy Garland — the girl who played Dorothy in *The Wizard of Oz* — once said:

> '*Always be a first-rate version of yourself, instead of a second-rate version of someone else.*'

The media constantly bombards us with images, telling us what we should look like and how we should act as teenagers. We end up all becoming lookalikes of each other. How boring is that?

'Always be a first-rate version of yourself, instead of a second-rate version of someone else.'

> > >

7

## you are UNIQUE . . .

That girl I loved on TV — Molly — affected my dress sense, big time! I remember conning my nanna into making me a copy of a bright jumpsuit that Molly wore. I even put 'Molly's' bright clips in my hair. (The mental images frighten me to this day!)

Sure, I went around dressed as 'Molly' for a while, but it wasn't the real me. I was just trying to copy someone else I admired.

Trends and fashions may come and go, but don't just buy something or wear an outfit because you are trying to be something you are not. You'll just end up being very uncomfortable because you're not being real to yourself.

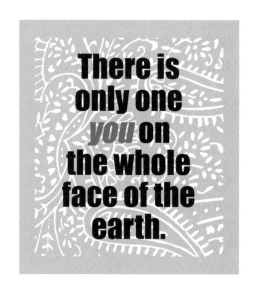

There is only one *you* on the whole face of the earth.

# get real!

## . . . the REAL YOU is amazing, lovable, a true diamond

Diamonds have it tough at birth!

They start out as grubby, dirty charcoal. Not pretty, any way you look at them. Someone has to clean them, polish them up so we can see what's so cool inside.

We need a bit of that clean and polish as well. Sometimes we need to rub away at the surface to enable our own unique diamond to shine.

At birth, you are a unique diamond, a true star who can achieve great things. As we get older, it's easy to forget that we must rub away some of the charcoal to find the true gem!

**wise words**

'Pure gold put in the fire comes out of it proved pure; genuine faith put through this suffering comes out proved genuine.'

1 Peter 1:7

**We must rub away some of the charcoal to find the true gem!**

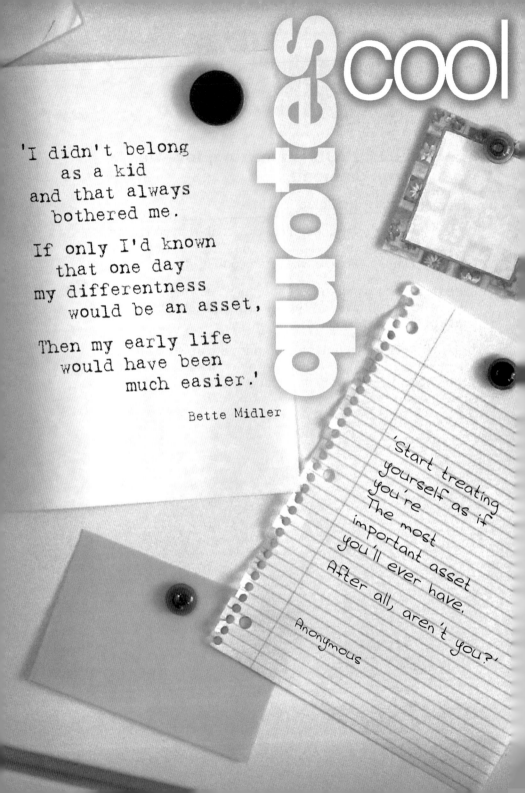

cool quotes

'I didn't belong
    as a kid
and that always
    bothered me.

If only I'd known
    that one day
my differentness
    would be an asset,

Then my early life
    would have been
        much easier.'

Bette Midler

'Start treating
yourself as if
you're
The most
important asset
you'll ever have.
After all, aren't you?'

Anonymous

# no one can make you feel **bad** *about* yourself . . .

Imagine this. You come to school, feeling pretty good about yourself. Then, someone says eight words that change everything:

*'Hey, what have you done to your hair?'*

You must make a decision, right then. Do you take this on board? Do you carry it around all day, feeling down because someone made a comment about your new hair colour? (YES this is the new shade of purple!)

Or do you say to yourself: 'Yep, my hair looks great! I'm happy to experiment with purple this week. It's only hair. If I don't love it, I simply have the power to change it.'

**'Someone else's opinion of you is none of your business.'** *Author unknown*

It's true, but a hard concept to grasp. We often allow others to dictate how we feel about ourselves. Frankly, if people **must** have an opinion of you all the time (and worse still, let you and others know what their opinion about you is), they obviously have far too much time on their hands! Remember, the only person who has the right to have an opinion about you is **you**! What **you** think of **you** is really the only opinion that matters.

**'Someone else's opinion of you is none of your business.'**

**Author unknown**

*'No one can make you feel inferior, without your consent.'*
*Eleanor Roosevelt*

11

Why would you allow

yourself to be bullied

. . . especially by

your own SELF?

# are you bULLYing yourself?

## . . . what am I hearing?

What does your own self-talk sound like?
Do you constantly talk to yourself using phrases like:

*'You idiot!'*

*'You're hopeless!'*

*'You've done it again!'*

*'Everyone hates you!'*

If you do, smack yourself over your head! Yes, I mean it!
You are bullying yourself and it is time to stop. I'm sure if
your friend was being bullied in front of you, you'd soon
step in and say something.
So why, then, would you allow
yourself to be bullied, especially
by your own SELF?

Instead, change your self-talk
into positive talk.

Talk to yourself in a positive way,
using words and phrases that
build you up rather than tear
you down.

### food for thought . . .

**There is only one you!**

**You are beautifully
and perfectly made.**

**When you get that,
you'll begin to
develop into a
more powerful and
lovable you.**

"+"  "+"  "+"

# it's time to fall in Love

## . . . with yourself

Let's face it. Watching *OC* re-runs and dreaming of your one true love is a bit of a waste of time . . . if you don't first learn to truly love yourself! People will be totally drawn to you as a person when you really like and love yourself.

I know what you're thinking here. If I love myself, that's:

a. *Weird, and*

b. *Won't everyone think I'm totally self-absorbed?*

No, that is not what I'm talking about. There is a huge difference between loving yourself, and being a boastful pain in the butt! People who like themselves are generally much happier people to be around. Have you ever been around someone who constantly says things like:

> **People will be totally drawn to you as a person when you really like and love yourself.**

'My hair looks terrible.'

'My butt looks huge in these jeans.'

'I'm hopeless at that!'

They're always saying negative things about themselves, usually because they want people around them to react and say things like:

'No, you look so great.'

'No, your butt looks really small in those jeans.'

'No you're not useless.'

After a while, people like this — who always speak negatively about themselves — can be plain exhausting to be around. You're a much nicer person to be around when you are happy with YOU. **Trust me!**

# Self esteem

## . . . no problem having a dose of this!

Self-esteem refers to our own feelings of self-worth or the esteem we give ourselves. It's a good thing. In fact, a healthy self-esteem — feeling good about yourself — will reflect on and translate to other people around you.

People with a healthy self-esteem, or self-image, tend to be pretty comfortable with themselves. They know what their strengths are and they understand that they are unique and valued.

People with a low self-image are usually easy to spot. They will usually be those people complaining that they are 'hopeless at this or that', 'aren't as beautiful as Sarah' or 'as cool as Jack'. They are, more often than not, the people who will gossip, put others down, talk negatively about others or will be a bully.

Developing a healthy self-image is one of the most important goals you can concentrate on right now. With a healthy self-image, you can accomplish anything you set your mind to! If you can do all that you can to work on your self-image as a teenager, you stand a much greater chance of becoming a happy and successful adult!

> **Developing a healthy self-image is one of the most important goals you can concentrate on right now.**

Continually check in

with yourself and see how

well your self-esteem bank

account is going.

# let's talk banking

## . . . how's your self-esteem account?

Everyone has what I like to call a **self-esteem bank account**. I guess you would liken it to your current account. You deposit money into your account, and you make withdrawals when you need to. If you don't have enough funds in your bank account, however, your request will be declined.

You see, you need to always make sure you deposit money, not just make withdrawals.

We all have a self-esteem bank account. When someone pays us a compliment or we receive a great score on a maths test, points are automatically deposited into our self-esteem account. When **you** pay someone a compliment or encourage someone else, you also make a deposit into **your** account. Why? Because doing something good for someone else also has the added bonus of making **you** feel good about yourself.

It's important to continually check in with yourself and see how well your self-esteem bank account is going. Right now, for example, are you currently in credit or debit? You can determine best what the balance of your account looks like by how you currently feel about yourself. Do you feel good about yourself, or do you require a bit more support and encouragement?

It also pays to have extra funds saved and sitting in your account, ready to dip into on a bad day.

> **Doing something good for someone else also has the added bonus of making _you_ feel good about yourself.**

>>>

17

# let's talk banking

The reason we all need to have a healthy self-esteem bank balance is for the occasions when we don't feel too good about ourselves or when someone says something negative or puts us down. Perhaps you get a poor grade for an English essay. Yes, this may make you feel pretty bad at that moment, but you have enough self-esteem points in your account to pick yourself up and say:

*'I'm okay'*

*'I matter'*

*'I'm amazing'*

*'This does not define who I am!'*

Withdrawals

Deposits

Balance

10.00

99.35

90.00

100.13

10.1

55.

20.0

16.57

13

.13

.56

# character

## . . . the person you are when no one is watching . . . that is your true character

It is the thing that defines you as a person. For example, do you talk about others in a negative way when they are not around, then be nice and friendly to them in person? That would make you a gossiping person, someone with the character of a 'gossip'.

Your character traits are the things that define and describe you.

How would your friends and family describe you?

Examples of character traits include:

- *honest*
- *caring*
- *encouraging*
- *determined*
- *hard working*
- *reliable*
- *friendly*
- *thoughtful*
- *grateful*
- *gutsy*

What qualities do you have that would describe your character?

It all comes down to

what you actually *do*,

not just what you say . . .

# integrity

My 10-year-old son loves football! On a family holiday once, his eyes caught sight of a ball in a shop and he just had to have it.

'Hey Mum,' he said. 'Can I go and buy that ball? I've got my pocket money with me.'

'Okay,' I said. 'We'll wait out here for you.'

A few minutes later, he emerged with **two** purchases — one was the football, the other a tasty chocolate bar. My first thought was to discipline him, suggesting that he might have thought to buy something for his sister with his loose change and not just think of himself.

'Mum, guess what—' (This will be a good one, I thought.) 'The lady in the store was going to charge me £2.95 for the football. But I remembered that it was actually £3.95.

'I told her too,' my son explained. 'And she was really impressed, "Well aren't you an honest boy!" she told me. "For that, you can have a chocolate bar as your reward!"'

**WISE WORDS**

*'If you're honest in small things, you'll be honest in big things.'*

*Luke 16:10*

My son showed integrity and he was rewarded for it.

Integrity is the word that describes your honesty and values. It is what defines you as an honest and reliable person, a person whose actions match their words. We all want to be seen by others as people of integrity — it all comes down to what you actually **do**, not just what you say.

That day, when my son showed integrity, it made me proud to be his mother. I told him that he had proved to himself that he was an honest person, by word and actions. It would have been quite easy for him to have purchased the ball at the lesser price offered — who would have known?

> > >

# integrity

Imagine you have arrived at your school drama class. The moment you get to your seat, you get a sinking feeling: 'Oh no, I watched that movie again last night and I've forgotten to do the homework for today!'

Now you might be a bit of a legend. You might even be the star student. You just can't believe that you let the homework slide this one time.

Then comes the worst thing a teacher can ever utter in such a circumstance: 'Where's your homework?'

(Honesty will mean detention.)

*'Moral character makes for smooth traveling; an evil life is a hard life.'*

Proverbs 11:5

'Um, oh Miss, I did do it,' you reply. 'It's sitting on my desk at home, really! I just forgot to bring it in today.'

'Miss' looks you in the eye, pauses for a moment and then says you can have an extra day to bring it to school — 'because we all know you are a trustworthy student. Besides, you usually have your homework completed.'

Now this is an example of your personal integrity at work! Your teacher has come to know you as a responsible and honest person. By lying, however, you have put your personal integrity at risk. Your integrity would be much more intact had you told the teacher the truth about not completing your set task. That simple act of honesty, though painful, would have reinforced to your teacher that you are a truthful and trustworthy person.

food for thought . . .

**Next time you are faced with a dilemma involving honesty, think of your integrity and follow your heart!**

# praise yourself

## . . . you're no loser

That's right! Just as you can bully yourself with negative thoughts, you can also build yourself up by praising yourself for all the great things that you do.

Praise yourself that you are trying hard at school. Praise yourself when you offer to help someone with a maths problem. Be kind to yourself because you are doing the best job that you can!

You may say it is hard to praise yourself for anything at the moment because you feel like such a 'loser'. Well, the very fact that you are reading this right now means that you are on the road to being a better you! You are an amazing, unique individual that is just bursting with potential. Believe this about yourself.

I do!

> **You are an amazing, unique individual that is just bursting with potential. Believe this about yourself.**

Affirmations are great tools
for you to encourage yourself
daily as you go through the
journey of 'teenage-hood'.

# affirmations

Affirmations are great tools for you to encourage yourself daily as you go through the journey of 'teenage-hood'.

It's a bit like having your own personal cheer squad in words. Affirmations have long been used by people wanting to achieve their goals. Affirmations are statements that you want to believe in or say to yourself — over and over again, so that your mind really grabs hold of them.

Examples may include:

- *'I am successful.'*
- *'I can do anything I set my mind to.'*
- *'I choose to be happy.'*
- *'I am a great friend to others.'*
- *'When I speak, I will only say positive things to others.'*
- *'I am a highly organised person.'*
- *'I am capable of winning the cross country.'*
- *'I am capable of achieving higher grades in maths.'*
- *'I am amazing.'*
- *'I am beautiful and I allow others to see my inner beauty.'*
- *'I am a person that people want to be friends with.'*

You can write out some of your own affirmations relating to your present goals and the person you want to be. Write or type them up on pieces of paper or card. Make sure they are clear enough to be able to read easily.

> > >

# affirmations

Stick these where you will see them daily:

- On your bathroom mirror.

- On the toilet door.

- On your bedroom wall (or better still, on the ceiling above your bed so you can see them just before you go to sleep at night and again first thing in the morning when you wake).

- In your diary or folders.

- On your bedroom door.

**Say these affirmations out loud every day until you really believe them with your heart.**

# cool **quotes**

' Believe in the best,

Think your best,

Study your best,

Have a goal for the best,

Never be satisfied with
less than your best,

Try your best,

And in the long run

Things will turn out
for the best. '

Henry Ford

'It's not what
you are that
holds you
back, it's what
you think you
are not.'

Dennis Waitley

'Believe you can
and you can.
Belief is one
of the most powerful
of all problem solvers.
When you believe that
a difficulty can be overcome,
You are more than halfway
to victory over it already.'

Norman Vincent Peale

'All the strength you need
to achieve anything
is within you.'
**Sara Henderson**

It doesn't cost anything

to treat others with respect

and kindness,

no matter who they are . . .

# treat others well

## . . . what goes around . . .

It doesn't cost anything to treat others with respect and kindness, no matter who they are. You should always be 'the bigger person' and treat others as you would like to be treated. That even means being nice to a replacement teacher coming into your classroom for the day, or the person delivering your mail. Always treat people respectfully. This principle ensures that kindness and respect will come back your way: 'What goes around comes around.'

> **'Love others as well as you love yourself. There is no other commandment that ranks with these.'** *Mark 12:31*

It's so important that you treat each other well. This is such an important principle to learn. You also need to remember that if you treat people well, they just might remember you when it comes to looking for employment or needing a favour.

When faced with any kind of interaction with someone else, you will always have a choice. You can treat the person with respect and kindness, or you can pretend that they do not really matter. Perhaps you don't even know the person.

It doesn't have to be that person in particular who returns your kindness, but you can be certain that you will be treated exactly as you treat others.

*'Don't pick on people, jump on their failures, criticize their faults – unless, of course, you want the same treatment.'*

*Matthew 7:1–2*

# think positive!

**Our thoughts**

**really do equal**

**our reality . . .**

# thOUghtS matter

two // think positive!

## . . . get a hold of yourself

Here's a scary thought. Just imagine for a minute that every single thought you have, from now on, will be heard by everybody around you. Your every fleeting thought is going to have a little loudspeaker attached that blasts to everyone around you!

Now picture yourself walking past a friend who is wearing a pretty garish top. You think to yourself:

> *'Oh boy, Sarah's looking awful today.*
> *She has no dress sense whatsoever.'*

Sarah hears your thought. She looks at you immediately, wounded by your insensitive and hurtful words. Now how do you feel? Pretty horrible?

Well the truth is, our thoughts really **do** equal our reality. In other words, the thoughts you have will come out, somehow. If you think something about a person, it will come out in some way, whether you are aware of it or not. Subconsciously, your negative thoughts or 'vibes' will project onto others.

Have you ever heard negative gossip about another person? As much as you try to ignore it, the next time you see that person you cannot help but be affected by those thoughts. You will act differently towards that person because of what you have heard.

Begin to control your thoughts. They are very strong and powerful! >>>

she says . . .

**'You can change your life in a moment if you change your thoughts and words.'**

**Ingrid Peskops**

# thoughtS matter

If you find yourself thinking something negative about another person, **STOP YOURSELF!** Try turning that negative into a positive.

For example, instead of thinking to yourself:

*'Oh boy, Sarah's looking awful today. She has no dress sense whatsoever.'*

Try changing your thought to:

*'Wow, Sarah sure is wearing an interesting top. She must have a pretty great self-image to wear whatever she wants, despite it not being what others are wearing or what is trendy.'*

Now, changing how we think about others is one thing that works. It's also true for thoughts about ourselves. If you continue to think you are a failure (or you're ugly, dumb, unpopular, hopeless at science, etc.), then it becomes true. Those thoughts will become your reality. It is pretty amazing, but true.

Whatever you consistently think about will be your reality! If you think you will fail that maths test and you continue to tell yourself how useless you are at maths, do you honestly think you can achieve success? Hardly! But try telling yourself the opposite:

*'Maths is such a challenge for me at the moment but I have the choice to not accept failure. What I can do is seek out extra help from my friends who are good at maths, or my teacher. Maybe I could even chat to Mum and Dad about getting a maths tutor. Either way, I can only improve from where I am at right now. For that next maths test, I am going to do brilliantly!'*

**American Indian
Rolling Thunder said:**

'People have to be
responsible for their
thoughts, so they have
to learn to control them.
It may not be easy, but it
can be done. First of all, if
we don't want to think certain
things, we don't say them. We
don't have to eat everything we see, and we
don't have to say everything we think. So we
begin by watching our words and speak with
good purpose only.'

good thinking . . .

**Practise changing
your thoughts from
now on.**

**You will be amazed
at the change in your
attitude.**

# TONIGHT'S FIGHTS!

| | | |
|---:|:---:|:---|
| I'm a failure | Vs | I'm getting better at this |
| I'm dumb | Vs | I am learning from my mistakes |
| I stuffed up | Vs | What a great opportunity to learn! |

# negative stuff

**thinking your way downhill...**

Who do I think I am?

I'm not pretty enough!

I'm useless.

I have nothing to offer.

I'm ugly.

I have no friends.

I'll never pass that test.

I stuffed up!

I'm hopeless at spelling.

I can't do it.

I'm a failure.

I'll never get any better.

I'm hopeless.

I'm a disappointment.

I'm dumb.

I'm not smart enough.

I don't know where to start!

Everyone's better than me.

**downhill**

## the way it's meant to be...

I can do better next time.

I am very capable.

I am gorgeous.

I have a lot to offer.

People like and accept me.

I am smart.

I will ask for help so I can pass the next maths test.

I will take this as an opportunity to learn.

I made a mistake but I've learnt from it.

Just because it didn't work out this time, it doesn't mean it won't next time!

I'm getting better at this.

I am learning from my mistakes.

What a great opportunity to learn!

Now I know what I need to work on to improve!

I am me and that is fantastic!

There is only one me and that's great!

I need to give people the opportunity to get to know me a little better.

positive stuff

# act 'as if'. . .

## . . . playing mind games

One of the amazing things about our mind is that it cannot distinguish between what we pretend is true and what is actually true. Pretty amazing, hey? This means that if we tell ourselves constantly that we are failures and hopeless, our minds will believe our thoughts and act as if we are failures. Our brains will send off signals to our bodies to make us feel tired, lethargic and sad, because these are the feelings that we are sending.

Have you noticed that when someone tells you something negative, you automatically feel down, lethargic and doubt yourself? When someone pays you a compliment, however, you generally feel happy, encouraged and your self-image soars!

One of the amazing things about our minds, is we can play tricks on it! Try acting 'as if'! This means that you act **as if** you are a happy, contented and amazing teen. Your mind will believe exactly what you tell it to. Act **as if** you are amazing and watch your body and mind tune into what you are acting.

Try this. Next time you go into a maths class, act **as if** you are a great mathematician and that maths problems come easily to you. Even if you find a problem confusing, you are acting **as if** you can accomplish it. It will make all the difference.

Or try this example. If you feel you are lacking friends, try acting **as if** you have many friends when you are next at school. When you arrive, act **as if** you have an abundance of friends, that you are well liked and that you enjoy spending time with people. As soon as you act **as if**, people are drawn to you. Your whole image will transform into one that is confident and happy because you are telling yourself that you are worthwhile as a friend. Just remember, your mind will believe what you tell it and will act accordingly.

# you are a magnet

Think of yourself as a magnet, a big one! (Just bear with me for a second on this one!)

You see, we attract in life what we dream and think about the most. If you want to achieve great things in your life, you have to first of all dream it and believe that you can achieve it, no matter what. This is called **faith**!

It's not enough to simply say, 'I want to pass my GCSEs'. You need to first dream that you will pass your GCSEs and believe that you are capable and will indeed achieve a good grades.

We attract in life what we believe about ourselves and our situations.

If you say, 'I'm not attractive,' you won't be! It's as simple as that. You are what you believe you are. If you say that you will fail, you will!

For example, think about the last time you went out and purchased a new outfit — maybe it was a nice top or a great dress or jacket. The first time you wear it out, you can't wait! When you meet up with people, they say, 'Hey, you look great today. You look really cool.' You feel really good about yourself and others respond to that feeling. It's not because of the actual item of clothing you are wearing, but it's because of the **feeling** that you are projecting.

When you feel good about yourself, positive, attractive, confident: these are the attributes that reflect from you.

Have you ever noticed, when you feel good about yourself, other people become very nice?

If you walk around with a sour look on your face all the time, guess what will look back at you? Yep! You guessed it!

**Try smiling at everyone and watch them smile back at you. It's contagious!**

# the **bLame** game

## . . . 'It's not my fault, EVER!'

Some people go through life blaming everyone else for the things that go wrong. All this does is give your power away to **other** people and situations. Stop blaming others and situations. It actually does not help. You can and should choose your reactions and take responsibility for things that you need to.

**Example:**

> 'My teacher gave me a "D" for that essay.' (whinge, whinge)

No! You probably earned a 'D' by leaving it until the last minute or not following instructions properly.

> 'Mrs Dale gave me a detention for spitting in the corridor! She's so mean!'

No! You earned that detention as a direct consequence of your actions.

People and situations do not just happen. They are often the result of our choices and the consequences of our actions.

True, sometimes other people's actions cause consequences that affect us. But it's important to direct the blame away from others. **Make a choice to not concern yourself with things you cannot change, and just consider the things you can!**

# the **rubber band**
## technique

### . . . **flick your way to self-control**

Try this! Place a rubber band or hair band around your wrist for one week. (Of course, I am expecting you will not make it tight! We are not trying to remove your favourite limb with this exercise!)

Okay, now each time you find yourself having a negative thought, flick the rubber band! I mean flick it so it stings!

Do this each time you catch yourself out having a negative thought about yourself. Flick it, also, when you have a negative thought about another person or a situation.

What you are going to learn is that you **can** control your thoughts. Try this experiment and watch how your thoughts soon change!

**You *can* control your thoughts.**

# you always have a **CHOICE**

## . . . the alternative to being a 'crazy lunatic'

One of the great things we humans share is the in-built capacity to make choices — real decisions about almost anything. We do not, however, always use these choices to our best advantage.

You see, good and bad things will always be thrown at us during many stages of our lives, but it is how we **choose** to react that makes all the difference!

Imagine, for example, that you spill a glass of cola all over the drawing you have just completed for art homework. You can **choose** to jump up, scream, tear up the drawing and run around the house like a crazy lunatic . . . **OR** you could choose to stop (scream if you need to), take a deep breath and leave the room for a minute. You could then choose to wipe off your drawing, and ask Mum or Dad to write a note to your teacher explaining the accident. Your parents might even consider writing a note seeking an extension. You see, it is all in how you choose to respond and how you choose to **see** a situation. Events, both good and terrible, will always happen; you just need to remember that you always have a choice as to how you will think and  >>> react!

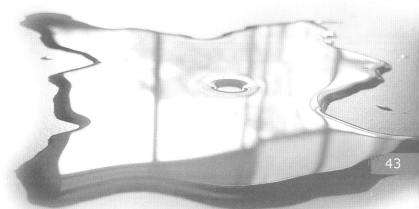

If a referee makes a poor call in your football match, and you disagree, you could launch into a tirade of abuse. You could choose to argue. You could choose to have a poor attitude towards the ref. You could, alternatively, choose to accept his decision without complaining, understanding that the ref is only human and is quite capable of making mistakes!

A student once said to me, 'You're always so happy in class Mrs Witt! Why are you always smiling?' My reply is always the same: 'Well, when I come to class, I usually make a choice to be happy and put on a smile, no matter what else might be going on.' If I am in a bad mood or over-tired, I must make a conscious choice that I am not going to reflect this onto others.

Next time you are faced with a reaction, pause for a moment and make a decision for yourself — how will you choose to react? And remember, your choices often have a knock-on effect on others.

**While we cannot always choose our situation or circumstances, we can always choose our response!**

'If you want people to
be glad to meet you,
you must first be glad
to meet them,
and show it.'

**Johann von Goethe**

'Worry is the
number one
killer of dreams,
achievement,
energy and
vitality.'

Jim Rohn

quotes

'Human character
is formed
not in the absence
of difficulty
but in our response
to the difficulty.'

**Jim Rohn**

**Mistakes are**

**moments**

**you learn from!**

# why failure is good

*'Insanity: doing the same thing over and over again and expecting different results.'*
Albert Einstein (1879–1955)

Despite what you have grown up to believe so far, failure is not a negative thing! Such inevitable setbacks in life are, quite simply, opportunities for you to learn.

Mistakes are moments you learn from! Failures are only negative if you ignore the lessons you could have learnt from them, repeating the same errors.

Many of us can go through life beating ourselves up every time we make a **mistake** or error of judgement. It is true that a mistake can be better described as a **mis-take**. Quite simply, this means we need to have another go! It means we missed the first time and it didn't quite work out the way we expected. But next time, we will do a second take and try again for a much better result.

Let's face it, we **ALL** make mistakes throughout our lives. We wouldn't be human if we didn't. As teens, such mistakes just seem worse at the time because we are trying out so many new things. Our bodies and emotions are all over the place and we have many pressures at school to achieve well, work hard and achieve good results. I want you, however, to retrain your >>>

## 'lessens'...

**'That's the reason they're called lessons,' the Gryphon remarked: 'because they lessen from day to day.'**

Lewis Carroll
*Alice's Adventures in Wonderland,*
Collectors Library, 2009.
First published 1865.

thoughts about mistakes and failures. Each time you make a **mis-take** or fail a test or forget to complete a piece of homework, say to yourself:

*'I am not perfect, but I am trying.'*

*'I made a mistake on this occasion, but I can only learn from that and grow as a person. It's in the past as of now and I can turn this negative into a positive by learning the lesson and doing better next time.'*

**Thomas Edison** (1847–1931) — inventor of a long-lasting light bulb — did not have an easy road to success. He made 1,200 mistakes — or failures — trying to make a little metal filament glow correctly inside a bulb. Eventually he succeeded. Just imagine if he had decided to give up even after the 50th failure. What he had, however, was the absolute belief in himself that eventually he would achieve success. He looked on each failed attempt not as a negative but as one step closer to finally achieving success with a functional light bulb.

Failure is, we learn from Edison, just a part of your success.

Australian inventor, **Professor Graeme Clark** AC, developed the bionic ear or cochlear implant in 1978 after a string of experiments and failures. People doubted what he said he could achieve.

Imagine if he'd listened to those people and given up?

Today, over 50,000 people across the world can hear because Professor Clark refused to give up!

## what do they know?...

Never listen to others who say you
cannot do something or that you
will never achieve success. If you
have belief in yourself, you will be
unstoppable and there will be no limit
to what you can achieve! Imagine
how many times Thomas Edison must
have been told 'You'll never get it!
Give up, Tom.'

# become a teen with passion!

**What makes your**

**soul sing?**

# find your **passion**

> *'Great dancers are not great because of their technique, they are great because of their passion.'*
>
> Martha Graham (1894–1991)

Being a teenager can definitely be tough at times — draining actually. There are so many demands on your time and mind; your body is growing at such a fast rate that it is virtually impossible to keep up with. **So it is essential that you find your passion!**

'But I'm not passionate about anything, except maybe sleep!' I hear you say. That's a pretty normal response from many teens. It is, however, really **REALLY** important that you seek out one or two things that you really enjoy doing — your passion.

Your passion is the thing you like to do that gives you a sense of satisfaction or joy. What makes your soul sing? You don't have to be brilliant at it, or even an expert for it to be your passion.

When you are pursuing your passion, you also get the added bonus of making deposits into your self-esteem bank account. It also makes you feel good because your body emits loads of endorphins (natural chemicals in your brain that make you feel good). It will make you feel great about yourself. >>>

# examples of
# passions

drawing

singing

learning to play
an instrument

painting

building things

volunteering

aerobics

bike riding

surfing

hiking

card making

designing

camping

gardening

clothes

playing in a band

watching movies

swimming

making jewellery

writing stories

sewing

scrap booking

painting miniature
figurines

shopping

keeping fit

cooking

dancing

skating

writing poetry

working with
your dad

acting

leading youth group

'It's not what
you are
that holds
you back,
it's what you
think
you are not.'

Dennis Waitley

'Learn to work
harder on
yourself
than
anything else.'

Jim Rohn

'All the strength
you need to
achieve anything is
within you.'

Sara Henderson

quotes

If there is chaos everywhere,

chances are . . .

life is pretty hectic

and confusing.

# get Organised!

Imagine walking into a doctor's surgery and having to step over a pile of papers, books, rubbish and clothes just to reach the examination chair. I'm guessing you would get the impression that the doctor was not too serious about being a doctor and looking professional. You would probably be wondering what kind of doctor he actually was!

In life, we need to have some sort of system to get organised, otherwise we tend to feel a bit out of control and not sure what we should be doing next. You can tell a lot about a teenager by the state of their bedroom at home! If there is chaos everywhere, chances are they also feel their life is pretty hectic and confusing.

You can begin to organise your life better today. You can start by organising your bedroom at home. Set aside an afternoon (or a whole week if it's that bad!) to find a home for all your possessions. You can buy inexpensive boxes or plastic containers from a local discount shop, or even cover some old shoe boxes in fun paper. Then get labelling!

Make sure you label your boxes clearly so that you know where to find things when you need them.

Things you can organise into boxes:

- Photographs
- School projects
- Make-up
- CDs and other disks
- Letters and cards from friends and family
- Keepsakes, journals, etc

# get organised!

You'll feel so much better once you begin to organise yourself. Some people are not naturally able to organise themselves in this way, and that's okay. It can seem like such a huge job that you don't know where to start. Why not ask your family or a couple of close friends to help you out for a day?

## Get yourself a funky diary.

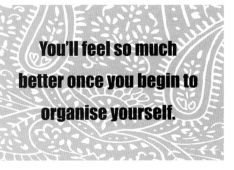

If you don't have one already, get yourself a cool diary. This is one of the best tools to help you get organised, especially for school or work. For school, you can use different coloured markers to label different homework subjects and set assignments. As you go, you can tick off work when it has been completed.

**You'll feel so much better once you begin to organise yourself.**

# develop an
# attitude
## of gratitude

**You are Blessed!**

If you woke up this morning with more health than illness,
You are more blessed
　　than the million who will not survive this week.

If you have never experienced the danger of battle,
the loneliness of imprisonment, the agony of torture
or the pangs of starvation,
　　You are ahead of 500 million people in the world.

If you can attend a church meeting without fear of
harassment, arrest, torture or death,
　　You are more blessed than 3 billion people in the world.

If you have food in the fridge, clothes on your back, a roof
overhead and a place to sleep,
　　You are richer than 75% of the world.

If you have money in the bank, in your wallet and spare
change in a dish somewhere,
　　You are among the top 8% of the world's wealthy.

If your parents are still alive and married,
　　You are very rare . . .

If you can read this,
　　You are more blessed than over 2 billion people in the
　　world who cannot read at all!

What goes around comes around . . .
Work like you don't need the money,
Love like you've never been hurt,
Dance like no one's watching,
Sing like no one's listening,
Live like it's heaven on earth!

Adapted from a text
by Stephen Eardley,
delivered at the
'Reconnections & New
Directions' Conference
in 2003.
(Lester B. Pearson College)

>>
59

# develop an **attitude** of gratitude

This passage has been on the back of my toilet door for about six years. Each time I read it, I am reminded how truly blessed I am! I also keep pocket-sized copies of it in a tin on the window sill in my toilet so people can take a copy home with them. It's very powerful, don't you think?

We are extremely fortunate in Western society to have unlimited potential within us, and the resources to achieve our dreams. There isn't anything that you could possibly dream up that you couldn't achieve with determination, locating the right resources and mentors, and a load of hard work.

As you grow into a responsible and amazing person, it is important that you always hold an **attitude** of **gratitude**. It is true that not all teens have wonderfully supportive families, a nice comfortable home or access to the finest education. Whatever your circumstances are right now, however, they do not determine your future. It is just your current situation.

### Your present reality does not equal your future success.

If you have clothing and access to food and shelter, you are extremely fortunate, and indeed wealthy — compared with millions of other people in the world right now. It does put things into perspective a bit doesn't it?

Learn to be grateful for each and every blessing that you have in your life, even if things do not feel much like a blessing right now. Just think, many of the hardships and failures you will experience along the way will just make you a stronger and more determined person. If your life seems pretty miserable at the moment — or things at home are awful — just be grateful anyway. It means that you will be even stronger as a person because you will have survived through tough times.

**the Bible says ...**

'Remember this: Whoever sows sparingly will also reap sparingly, and whoever sows generously will also reap generously.'
2 Corinthians 9:6 NIV

# begin a
# gratitude
## journal

A great way to really put the law of gratitude into place is to start a **Gratitude Journal**. You may find this a bit weird at the start and may even feel strange writing your thoughts down. Begin by writing just one thing that you are grateful for each day. It may even be that you are healthy or have the ability to write down something to be grateful for. The point is to start somewhere. You will soon find that you have a whole list of things for which to be grateful.

'People become really quite remarkable when they start thinking they can do things.

When they believe in themselves they have the first secret of success.

There are so many ways in which young people can work to make a difference.'

**Hugh Evans**
**Young Australian of**
**the Year recipient**

'All the things we achieve are things we have first of all imagined.'

David Malouf
Australian Writer

'Receiving a gift is like getting a rare gemstone; any way you look at it, you see beauty refracted

Proverbs 17:8

'Shoot for the moon.
Even if you miss it
You will land among the stars.'

Lester Louis Brown
American Journalist

# practise
# generosity

Have you ever given a gift — I mean something you **really** loved, an item you would want yourself — to someone else? It feels so good when you get to see the excitement and happiness on the other person's face.

I absolutely love giving gifts. I always feel so good when I do and definitely receive much more out of giving than I ever do from receiving. Giving is also a very quick 'pick-me-up'. Next time you are feeling a bit low or lost, give a gift to someone who looks like they need one.

Please note that a 'gift' does not have to cost money or even be a physical item that you could put on a shelf. You could write someone an encouraging letter or note. You could offer to baby-sit for a tired mum or dad. You could offer to help someone else study for a test or you could pick your mum some flowers from the garden. You will instantly feel great when you are generous with your thoughts and time. It also adds deposits into your own self-esteem account because you are giving of yourself.

The law of giving means that you will always receive a return 10 times more than you will ever give. But what you get back will not usually come from the people or places that you expected.

**wise words**

'Be especially careful when you are trying to be good so that you don't make a performance out of it. It might be good theatre, but the God who made you won't be applauding.'

*Matthew 6:1*

## food for thought . . .

Don't ever keep track of your generosity. The people who constantly keep a track of people whom they have served or blessed are painful. If you are going to expect people to do things for you in return, don't bother! Give without ever expecting.

63

# volunteer

## your time

When I started teaching, there were no paid positions available at the school I had attended as a teenager. It was my favourite school and I really wanted to work there. So I chose to volunteer my time two days every week, just to gain teaching experience. I really enjoyed those times and it reinforced to me that teaching was the profession I wanted to follow. Before long, I was offered casual work within the school. I gained a full-time position the following year because I had experience within the school and they knew me, by then, quite well.

In giving back to others, think about perhaps volunteering your time to help out others. Or consider working for specific organisations. Many places rely on volunteers to keep them operational. Not only does volunteering help out others, but the benefits to you can be immeasurable.

**Volunteering also increases your self-esteem because we build ourselves up when we help out others.**

At a youth forum I attended, a teenager aged 18 got up to talk about his experiences in volunteering. He was 12 years old when he first began offering help in a care home for the elderly. He really enjoyed his time there and made many friends while gaining valuable work experience.

When he decided to apply for a job at a major fast-food outlet, he wasn't alone. More than 700 young people had put their names down for about three positions. He thought he had no hope at all because he had never had a paid part-time job before. 'What chance have I got?' he thought.

The employers picked him. They had seen something he had missed in his moments of doubt — all the experience he had gained while volunteering at the care home. The skills he built up over six years had included working with people, problem solving, commitment to the position and residents, diligence and teamwork.

Think about some of the areas that you are interested in pursuing as a career when you leave school. Consider approaching some businesses in your area that relate to your interests. Many people in positions of importance began by volunteering their time. And don't think any job is beneath you.

Remember, everyone has to start somewhere. If you have to make coffee and clean up after other people just so you can be around when positions become available, then do so! Plenty of people began their careers as coffee servers who did so with a smile on their face and a 'can do' attitude.

**Be faithful in the small tasks, and people will trust you in the bigger tasks.**

**Accept help**

**when it is**

**offered to you . . .**

# be ready to
# receive

## . . . ask for help!

Imagine you are drowning in the ocean. A helicopter flies overhead, and a ladder hangs down, with a rescuer attached. What's the first thing you need to do in order to be rescued? That's right. You have to put your arms up! If you were bobbing up and down in the ocean with your arms firmly crossed across your chest, not only would you sink fairly quickly, but it would make it awfully difficult for you to be rescued.

So, ask for help! Accept it when it is offered to you. As soon as you are open to people being there for you and assisting you in life, they will show up and you will **succeed**. Trust me on this one!

You must **BELIEVE** that you will achieve your dreams and goals. You must participate in your rescue.

**You must participate in your rescue . . .**

# say **thank you,** often

**Question:** 'How much does it cost you to say "thank you" to someone?'

**Answer:** 'Absolutely nothing!'

One of the simplest principles of being thankful is so very often overlooked or forgotten. Say it!

Something that I really appreciate about my students is that they will often say 'thank you' to me at the end of a drama lesson. Whilst it costs nothing for students to thank me, it means a great deal to me because it shows that the person appreciates the effort I have put in to preparing a lesson.

Next time you step off a bus, thank the bus driver; that driver has reached your destination safely. If a teacher hands you back an exam or assignment that has been marked, say thank you because personal time has gone into marking it for you.

**A little thanks costs little, but is worth much.**

# thank your
# parents

## . . . as a teenager I rarely thanked my parents

The way I saw it, they had a duty to look after me since they chose to have me in the first place. That was, I now see, a rather ungrateful attitude.

Now that I am a parent, I realise what a selfish attitude I had.

I make a point to **always** thank my parents now.

### wise words

'Children, do what your parents tell you. This is only right. "Honour your father and mother" is the first commandment that has a promise attached to it, namely, "so you will live well and have a long life."'

Ephesians 6:1–3

# achieve awesome results!

**You CAN achieve**

**anything at all,**

**even if it seems impossible**

**at present!**

# you can **achieve** anything

## . . . don't stare at your present circumstances

It is true! You are in the driver's seat of your life and you **CAN** achieve anything at all, even if it seems impossible at present!

Do you remember when you were younger how you thought you could **be** anything you wanted to be when you grew up? Perhaps you wanted to be a fireman or an actress or maybe you wanted to be an acrobat in the circus. Well, you still can. The only thing that has changed from when you were young is your belief system. You believed you could actually do **anything** you wanted when you were young because no one said you could not.

When I was little, all I wanted to do was sing. I performed to everyone around me and loved putting on concerts for my neighbours. The only thing that stopped me putting out an album was that I decided I could not really do it after all. Now, I realise that you need a certain amount of talent to be a singer (and I must admit I am lacking a bit of that) but despite the lack of skills early on, I could have made a decision that I was going to be a singer. I could have enrolled in singing lessons, performed in a band and then recorded a CD. With modern technology, even people lacking talent can be made to sound like they have the voice of an angel! The point is, you can achieve the seemingly impossible.

73

That's what the doctors

thought of me, but the

main thing was

what I thought . . .

# licence to **dream**

**'You create your own universe as you go along.'**
*Winston Churchill*

American Morris Goodman was piloting his plane in 1981 when it crashed. He suffered traumatic injuries and was not expected to survive. The pilot's spinal chord was crushed, and he was completely paralysed. His entire diaphragm was crushed, he was unable to breathe on his own and he lost the ability to swallow. All he could do was blink his eyes. Doctors made the diagnosis that he would never walk again and he would not breathe without the aid of a ventilator. He would be a 'vegetable' for the rest of his life and would only be able to blink.

**'That's what the doctors thought of me, but the main thing was what I thought.'**
*Morris Goodman*

Morris made a decision in his hospital bed, despite being severely injured, that he would not accept the diagnosis.

He made a conscious decision that he would recover, and that he would walk out of the hospital at Christmas, some eight months later.

**'The only thing I had to work with in hospital was my mind.'**

He then focused on seeing himself as a normal, fully healed human being. He began to push his diaphragm, forcing it to move. The ventilator was eventually removed and doctors were amazed that he could breathe by himself. He then began to receive extensive therapy on his legs, eventually achieving his goal of miraculously walking out of the hospital by Christmas.

What does this have to do with being a happy and successful teenager?

>>>

## licence to **dream**

Well, if someone in that pilot's dire position could change his reality into something amazing — walking out of the hospital — you also can achieve anything you set your mind to. We don't realise the huge potential of our mind. We do not even use one tenth of our mind's true capacity.

Set your mind on your dreams. Picture yourself as successful and achieving amazing things and it will happen!

**You also can achieve anything you set your mind to.**

# what have you got to
# Lose?

*'Whether you think you can or you can't,
either way you are right.'* Henry Ford

You have absolutely nothing to lose by changing your thoughts and present behaviours and attitudes. If nothing changes, you have not lost anything, have you? You will be in exactly the same place as you were before. So believe in yourself!

You may be thinking, right now, that where you are is 'as good as it's gonna get', but the fact is you have the world at your feet right at this very moment. You need to take charge of your circumstances. If you are struggling with maths at school, this does not mean that you will always be hopeless with numbers. The fact is, your present circumstances indicate you are struggling with the subject, but you can make a choice to change that!

**Example:**

When I was a student at high school, I remember struggling with legal studies. I just did not get all the technical language and was not scoring good results at all. Unbeknown to me at the time, my legal studies teacher actually approached my mum. The teacher had seen that I was struggling and thought it would be a good idea to put my efforts elsewhere. My mother was told I should drop the subject but she chose to keep me in the dark on that one! I'm glad that she took a different view. She thought that I needed some encouragement to work harder. I listened and made a bigger effort to comprehend the information I was getting in class. I began writing out cue cards and sample essays. I soon began to understand the work a lot better and actually enjoyed the subject. I spent many evenings studying and revising my notes. By the end of the

>>>

## the places you will go...

**You have brains in your head
You have feet in your shoes.
You can steer yourself
Any direction you choose.**

**You're on your own.
And you know what you know.
And you're the guy
Who'll decide where to go.**

Dr Seuss, *Oh, the Places You'll Go!*,
HarperCollins, 2008.

year, my results had improved 30%! Now just imagine if I had been given the advice to give up.

Your circumstances might seem difficult at the moment, but you absolutely do have the power to change your future, right from this moment. If things are not working or you don't feel like you have any real direction, that is pretty normal for a teenager. The great news is that it can all change as soon as you make a decision that tomorrow will be different.

John Maxwell said that while you cannot go back to the beginning of your life and make a brand new start, you can start from now and make a 'brand new end'.

Just think what you could do and be if you just make a decision right now to change your future. Go on, give it a try!

## only you...

**Only you can make your mind up!**

**You're the one and only one!**

Dr Seuss, *Hunches in Bunches*,
HarperCollins, 2008.

# the power of setting goals

We can walk for what

    seems like an eternity and

not really get

    anywhere important . . .

# the power of
# setting goals

*'What you get by achieving your goals is not as important as what you become by achieving your goals.'*

*Zig Ziglar*

Imagine this. You are headed off on a school camp for a week. It's a hiking camp and you are really excited because you will be hiking with your friends and teacher for three solid days. You arrive at base camp, begin organising your hiking pack, then set off with your group for the three-day trek. You begin walking through the glorious countryside, and admire the beautiful scenery.

After about five hours, however, you wonder how far you have got to go before you get to your destination for the day to set up for camp.

You call to the teacher, 'When will we get to where we're going?'

'I don't know,' your teacher replies. 'I didn't bring a map. I just thought we'd keep walking until we stopped.'

I'm guessing that at that moment you would start feeling a little nervous and slightly anxious about where you are all heading. It may also be safe to assume that at that moment, you are totally lost!

Life can be like a long hike. We can walk for what seems like an eternity and not really get anywhere important. That is exactly why setting goals in life is of major importance. We need to have a clear map that we can follow and revise along the way when needed.

**Our map is the record of our future goals!**

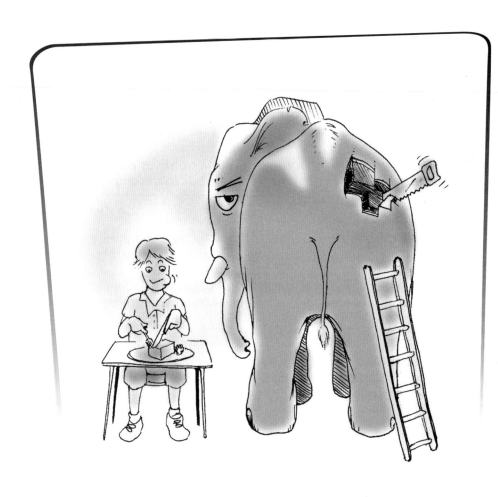

'How do you eat an elephant?

One bite at a time.'

AUTHOR UNKNOWN

# Why people don't set goals

**80% of life is knowing why**

**20% of life is knowing how**

There are some simple but powerful reasons why people will not set goals:

- *They don't understand the importance of setting goals.*

- *They have never set aside the time.*

- *They don't know how. (Some people think that just by thinking about getting better results in English, that it will automatically happen!)*

- *They are afraid of failing or being rejected by their friends or peers.*

Setting goals is basically like setting a road map for where you are heading. It helps to give you clear directions so that you can check in with yourself to make sure you are on track. Put even more simply, a goal is a dream with a date attached to it. >>>

**Setting goals is basically like setting a road map for where you are heading.**

**Example:**

You may decide that when you leave school you are going to work as a nurse and eventually become a midwife, helping deliver babies. Just say you are 14 years old now. You probably already have a bit more of an interest in science than your friends. You set yourself goals for the next few years along the following lines:

- *Get good results in science.*
- *Study biology and other science subjects at A level.*
- *Talk to your careers adviser at school about all the possible courses that are available to you to study nursing.*
- *Participate in work experience and volunteer work in a local hospital.*
- *Work hard to get the results you need to get into the nursing course that you desire.*
- *Begin nursing course.*
- *Complete nursing degree.*
- *Begin training in midwifery.*

A friend of mine, Dale Beaumont, describes goal setting as:

**'Deciding on the achievement of a specific objective sometime in the future because of a certain feeling which is obtained as a result of its accomplishment.'**

Goal setting is one of the most important practices you can learn as a teenager. You will need to be a goal setter if you want to achieve great things with your life. Otherwise, you risk being a drifter!

Your goal right now might be to become better organised, to work on homework for 45 minutes each night, to keep your bedroom tidy or to be a good friend to others. Whatever your goals are right now, make a commitment to turn them into reality, one step at a time. You do not have to see the entire journey, just take the first step in the direction you want to head. In other words, **'Take the first bite of the elephant!'**

**'If you aim at nothing,
you'll hit it every time.'**

Author unknown

'What you get by
achieving your goals
is not as important
as what you become
by achieving
your goals.'

Zig Ziglar

'The world is but a canvas
to our imaginations.'

Henry David Thoreau
American Essayist
and Poet

**Write goals down and**

**commit to seeing**

**them through . . .**

# Write down
## your goals

### . . . give them flight!

You give your goals wings when you write them down. That is because you make a commitment to what you want to work at and achieve next.

Maybe your goal is to pass all your end-of-year exams. Your goal sheet might look like this:

- *Find a study partner for English (hardest subject) and science (second most difficult).*

- *Offer to help someone else in maths (my best subject).*

- *Ask my English and science teachers for some practise exams so I can use these in my study time.*

- *Set aside Monday and Wednesday evenings for 1½ hours to revise content.*

- *Pass my exams!*

You can do this for any of your goals. The point is, you must write them down and commit to seeing them through. All successful people set clear goals. It is not rocket science. It is simply the way to get things done and achieve results.

It is also important to note that you should attach a date to each goal that you record. Write the dates in your diary if that helps. Attaching a date to your goals gives you a clear timeline for completing them. Make sure you write out a new one when you have achieved your goal.

'Take the first step in faith.

You don't have to see the

whole staircase,

just take the first step.'

Dr Martin Luther King (1929–1968)

# give yourself
# rewards

## . . . for achieving goals

There are times when working towards the goals you have set for yourself is just plain hard work. No one expects you to work and work and not get anything for it. True, you will experience great personal satisfaction from achieving your goals. It is also important, however, to give yourself the occasional reward. Here are just a few of the rewards you could give yourself for achieving goals along the way to your success:

- Treat yourself to a movie or night out.

- Give yourself one or two nights off completing work.

- Get tickets to see a favourite band close to when you expect to achieve a set goal.

- Plan a fun night in with a group of friends.

- Plan a shopping spree to buy new clothes when you achieve your goal.

If your goal is a fairly big one, don't get put off. Large goals are achieved by breaking them up into smaller, bite-sized, achievable pieces. It can be far too scary to tackle a goal that seems too big from the start. Begin by taking the first small step. Then, once that goal is achieved, take another step. Just keep going. You **will** get there in the end.

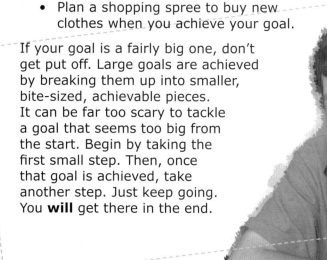

# revise your goals often

**. . . it is no use buying a new outfit and leaving it buried in the back of your wardrobe.**

Well, as silly as that sounds, such cobweb-attractive behaviour is exactly the point I want to make here about setting goals. You must check in with yourself often when it comes to setting goals. Do not simply get all enthusiastic, write out your goals and then bury the piece of paper in your bedroom for the next six months. (If your bedroom is in the same state as most teenagers', you may never ever find those goals again until the day you get married and move out of home!)

Put your goals somewhere that is clearly visible, daily. Do not write them on a scrappy piece of paper but type them up or make them at least look important. You may even like to laminate the page, put a magnet on the back and pop it on the fridge door! Better yet, blue tack it to the back of your toilet door so you are reminded daily what you are striving to achieve.

*You have 525,600 minutes in every year. How do you personally use them? Do you use them well?*

**Do not write them on a scrappy piece of paper but type them up or make them at least look important.**

# dream big!

**. . . in order to achieve anything great in life, we must first dream it.**

Imagine you would love to drive an amazingly fast, bright, shiny red Porsche. Try making that a goal without first picturing it in your mind. It's impossible, isn't it? That is the amazing thing about our minds. We cannot have a big goal or dream without first picturing it in our minds.

In order for us to create our dreams, we must first imagine them in our minds. We have, in fact, all been blessed with one of the most amazing creations in the form of our imaginations.

This means that we are totally free to lie awake in bed at night and dream the most amazing hopes and dreams for ourselves. Think for a moment about what you want to achieve in your life. Imagine for just a moment that you have no limitations. What would you dream for yourself?

It is important to have dreams, otherwise we do not have a clear idea of where we are headed. Set yourself time to really dream big! Then begin to put some time and energy into making those dreams a reality.

**Set yourself time to really dream big.**

Your dream book will help you

      to focus on the little things that

are all small steps in

      achieving your dreams . . .

# create a
# dream book

## . . . crazy colours — all part of a smart idea

A great activity you can do to help you realise your goals and dreams is to create a **Dream Book**. You can purchase a folder or scrapbook that you can decorate to represent you! Not only does creating a Dream Book cement your goals — because you have committed them to paper — but you also create a visual representation for what you aim to achieve.

If your goal, for example, is to become a successful, independent businesswoman, look through magazines and cut out a picture of a person who best represents that image for you. Type up words and phrases on your computer in crazy colours, cut them out and paste them in your Dream Book. Try words and phrases like:

- I am successful
- I am gorgeous
- I am friendly
- I will get 98% for my legal exam
- I have integrity
- Friends are drawn to me

If your goal is to become a police officer, cut out a picture of a police officer and paste it in your Dream Book. If your goal is improved health and fitness, paste in pictures of healthy people, healthy bodies and healthy foods.

**the places you will go . . .**

*Creating a 'Dream Board' can be just as good as a book or folder. You can purchase an inexpensive noticeboard, cover it in bright fabric or cool wrapping paper and pin pictures, words and phrases to it. Make sure you hang it somewhere clearly visible on a daily basis.*

Look at your dream book often! Just before you go to sleep each night is a good time to open it up. That is the time when it will encourage your subconscious to dream about your goals. Starting the day by flipping through your dream book each morning will also help you to focus more on the little things throughout each day that are all small steps in achieving your dreams.

Mentors are people

　who have usually gone before

you and are

　successful in their

　　chosen fields . . .

# seek out
# mentors

## . . . wise counsel from experienced people

Mentors are a bit like coaches for life. Mentors are people who have usually gone before you and are successful in their chosen fields. The most effective way to be a successful teen and achieve your goals is to seek out a mentor to help you along the way.

I believe that all teenagers need at least one mentor — someone from whom you can seek advice, and who will help you on your journey to success.

I was very fortunate, when I was a teenager, to have a couple in my church who were able to mentor me throughout my junior and middle school years. They kept an eye on me and were the two people I was able to turn to for advice and help if I was experiencing difficulty. That was especially helpful with issues relating to parents.

A mentor could be a teacher from your school, an older student, youth leader, church pastor, uncle, aunt, parent or grandparent. Someone you know and respect.

You can read books or speeches about people who have been successful in life. If you want to be a successful basketball player, seek out people who are either playing or have had previous success. Many elite sports players have produced an autobiography — a book that discusses their life story — or someone has written their biography. Books can be an amazing source of information and inspiration as to how someone has overcome hurdles and challenges and achieved success in their chosen field.

'Take good counsel and accept correction – that's the way to live wisely and well.'

*Proverbs 19:20*

>>>

# seek out mentors

And I would be very surprised if each successful person you followed did not have at least one great mentor from whom they learnt.

Write a letter to someone you admire and whose success you would like to emulate. You would probably be surprised that successful people are also normal, everyday people just like you. They have only achieved success because they were driven and set themselves clearly-defined goals. Many successful people get to be that way because they had great mentors in their lives to guide them. They would probably be more than happy to speak to you, or recommend some ideas and directions.

I remember, when I was about 16, wanting to be an actor. Kylie Minogue was then an actress on the hit television series, *Neighbours*. I wrote her a letter seeking advice on where I should go to get auditions and increase my potential to land an acting role.

I was really surprised when she wrote back with a brief note explaining how she had got her first 'big break' and made suggestions as to which production companies I should get in contact with.

Even though I was not successful in pursuing my television career (I had to be content with being a drama teacher), I was able to secure an agent and went on to work in television with bit-parts for four years.

Thanks Kylie!

**in Kylie's footsteps...**

**Kylie Minogue started somewhere. She had dreams and goals.**

**You need to start somewhere too, right now.**

# step out of your comfort zone and into your
# courage zone

**. . . let's be honest here. Sometimes it is pretty hard to step out and give new things a go.**

When we have a go at something new or unfamiliar to us, we risk looking stupid, feeling silly, failing in front of our friends or falling flat on our face. That's pretty much why so many people go through their lives achieving less than they are capable of. They are too afraid to try something new or too 'out there'.

To take on a new challenge or to learn a new skill often takes a great deal of courage. And it's not always easy. But think about this for a minute: what is the worst thing that can possibly happen if you step out and take a risk? Sure, you might not be successful, but so what!? Imagine for a minute that you have embarrassed yourself, or fallen flat on your face in front of your peers. How do you feel? Try and put yourself in that position for a moment. How do you really feel? Sad? Lonely? Is there a pit in your stomach?

So now that you've experienced what it might feel like to fail, you're still okay, right? You're still alive? Well that's the worst that can happen. You may feel a bit miserable for a short time, but you'll pick yourself up and get back out there and try again.

Okay, now that you've experienced that feeling, imagine that you have given something new a try and you have actually succeeded. How do you feel now?

For example, you've just scored the winning goal in your football match. I'm sure you feel pretty amazing.

>>>

## Step out of your comfort zone
## and into your courage zone

When I first began teaching, I had a huge fear of public speaking, and I mean massive! In my first year of teaching I recall being asked to stand in front of a group of parents to explain all the exciting things we had planned for their children for the year ahead. From the very moment I was told of that event, I felt sick, physically ill! What if they laughed at me? I thought. What if they thought I was so bad at speaking in front of them, that they thought I must be a hopeless teacher? What if they all pulled their kids out of our school based on my poor speech? What if I threw up in front of them (highly likely considering how afraid I was!)?

I recall that, on the day of the parent information evening, I could not eat at all and I stressed about what I would say to them and how it would be received.

During the meeting, I sat at the back with a colleague, trying to plan a last-minute escape. Could I fake a case of appendicitis? Could I collapse and get rushed to hospital? They would never ask me to speak again (hopefully).

**It's time to have a big dose of courage and step out of your comfort zone.**

Well, I did get up on that evening and give my five-minute speech. I am sure that I appeared pretty nervous and I probably spoke too fast. But the point is, I didn't pass out. No one pulled their kids out of the school because of my talk, and you know what? The next time it was much easier, and the next time even more so.

These days, if there is any opportunity to get up in front of others and give a speech, run an assembly or parents' meeting, guess who's the first one to put her hand up? Yep, you guessed it! One of the things I love doing the most these days is sharing information with students and parents. I love giving talks because I kept pushing myself out of my comfort zone early on and into my courage zone. Yes, it was scary, but the benefits far outweighed the short time that I had to feel scared and unsure about myself.

**It would be fairly easy to go through life experiencing things and barely stepping out of my comfort zone. But it takes courage to take on new challenges.**

Close your eyes again for a moment. Imagine all the things you would like to be able to achieve if you absolutely knew for certain that you could never fail. Now write them all down, as many as you can imagine. This gives them credibility; it makes them real. Now circle the goal that sticks out the most when you read back over the list. Put a date (a realistic one) next to it and get on with making this happen.

It's time to have a big dose of courage and step out of your comfort zone. You'll never achieve all of your dreams and your full potential unless you take a step forward in faith and show some real courage.

## Go on. You can do it!

# trying teen times

Teenage years

. . . life's big ER!

(Emotional Rollercoaster)

# emotional
# rollercoaster

## . . . this maths book is heading your way!

The 'ER' — life's big emotional rollercoaster called teenage years. Of all the teenagers I have spoken to, this syndrome is by far the most common complaint. And no wonder! Hormones (yes, there's that horrible word again) seem to be running out of control through your body. It is during these delightful teenage years that you can find yourself flying off the handle at anyone, for no apparent reason.

Once, you may have loved hanging out with your younger sister or brother, but you now find yourself hurling a tirade of abuse at them as soon as they dare to enter your bedroom! And your parents are by no means immune to this abuse. They will get yelled and screamed at just for asking how school was today; not so long ago, this perfectly normal type of question was acceptable and did not usually incur aggresive responses!

I remember when I was in secondary school, trying desperately to wade through my awful maths homework. My mum only had to slide open the bedroom door for me to launch a tirade of abuse about the horrors of school, life, maths, my brother, teachers . . . This angry outburst was usually capped off by a flying maths book aimed directly at the door! I often had Mum in tears over my unnecessary outbursts. I would feel awful afterwards but I just could not seem to control such feelings of anger and frustration.

**'The best way to cheer yourself up
is to cheer someone else up.'**

**Mark Twain**

'Some of the best lessons
we ever learn,
We learn from our mistakes
and our failures.
The error of the past
is the success
And wisdom of the future.'

Tyron Edwards

'Worry is just fear
painting pictures
in your mind.'

Jim Rohn

# don't be in such a *hurry*

**Ages 5 to 10:** You cannot wait to grow up, get to secondary school and gain a bit more freedom from your parents.

**11 and beyond:** Life can be demanding under the weight of school, home life, body burdens and all the extra responsibilities that are thrust on you. We can be in such a hurry to get through our teenage years so we can get our driving licences, turn 18, and finally be independent adults.

**STOP**

**Please, do not be in such a hurry to grow up!** Each season of your life has its ups and downs; challenges. But remember that you only get to be a teenager once, so choose to enjoy it. Do not choose to wish this time away!

Being a teen

can be a very

stressful time.

# stress

There is no doubt that being a teen can be a very stressful time. You are coping with huge changes including:

- School/homework pressures
- Body changes
- Physical changes
- Emotions
- Parents
- Friendships

It is really important that you find healthy outlets for dealing with any stress that you are feeling. Some people deal with stress by exercising or talking with friends. Make sure you find the outlet that best suits you, and make sure you take action.

One of the biggest stress indicators is illness, so make sure you take stress seriously and keep a healthy check on yourself.

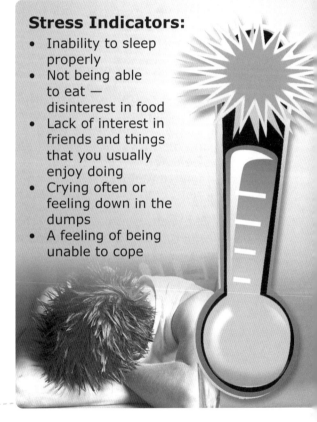

## Stress Indicators:

- Inability to sleep properly
- Not being able to eat — disinterest in food
- Lack of interest in friends and things that you usually enjoy doing
- Crying often or feeling down in the dumps
- A feeling of being unable to cope

If you have been struggling with any of the above symptoms for a few weeks or more, you could very well be struggling with stress. It is important that you talk with your parents, teacher or school counsellor. It would also be good to visit your doctor to get a thorough examination.

# stress **busters**

### . . . if you are feeling a bit stressed, try some of the following solutions . . .

- **Exercise.** This is great for relieving stress because when you exercise, your body releases its own natural 'feel good' chemicals. It also helps the blood flow better throughout your body, giving it a great boost.

- **Go for a long walk.** *(See above)*

- **Have a couple of early nights.** If you are stressed, this could be a sign that your body needs a bit of a rest. Make yourself a warm drink, grab a good book and read for a little while before having a good, long sleep. You need between 8 and 10 hours' sleep per night to feel well rested and stress-free. Make sleep a priority, and your other priorities will fall into place.

- **Eat well.** Fill your body with lots of fruit and vegetables. This may sound a bit boring, however, spending a few days giving your body extra minerals and vitamins will help restore you.

- **Hire your favourite comedy movie** (or chick flick if you are a girl!) from the DVD store! Laughter also releases your body's natural endorphins that help to make you feel better.

- **Do something you love doing**, e.g. paint, draw, write, hike, ride, or make something. What is your passion?

- **Spend a day out with friends**. Go shopping, hang out together.

# when you're
# feeling down

If you are feeling down for any length of time (e.g. two weeks or more), it is important that you seek help. Being a teen can be tough at the best of times and it is quite common to feel overwhelmed sometimes and unable to cope. These feelings, however, should not last more than a couple of days. If you consistently feel sad and hopeless about your situation, it is important that you ask for help.

Talk to your parents, teacher, friend, school counsellor, sister, brother, aunty or church/youth group leader. Tell them honestly how you are feeling. If you feel that this is too much for you to cope with, please call one of the numbers at the back of this book. Trained people can also give you confidential advice and assistance.

### signs of depression

- Feeling sad, hopeless
- Crying often for no apparent reason
- Feeling tired and exhausted all the time
- Extreme weight loss or weight gain
- Lack of motivation and feeling like you cannot be bothered
- Loss of interest in activities
- Feeling worried and anxious often
- Sleeping too much or feeling like you need to sleep all the time
- Turning to drugs or alcohol to cope with life
- Harming/cutting yourself

*If you experience two or three of these symptoms for more than a week or two, please seek help from an adult.*

Source: *www.beyondblue.com.au*

Life can be

overwhelming

for some people.

# what to do when friends say they want to **hurt** themselves

## . . . not a burden for your shoulders

Life can be overwhelming for some people. Reasons may include family issues at home, problems with siblings, weight issues, friendships or more serious matters of abuse. Whatever the issue, it is important to remember that they are issues that feel important to the person suffering them at the time.

A way of reacting to these feelings might involve people wanting to inflict pain on themselves. This is called **self-harm**. It may be cutting oneself lightly on the arm or leg to feel a sense of pain, or at the other extreme, could be as final and shocking as suicide.

If a friend comes to you about self-harm, or you are aware that a person is harming himself or herself in some way, it is important that you let an adult know. This is a heavy burden for anyone to handle, let alone a teenager, so make sure you tell an adult, no matter how difficult it may seem. If you let your mum or teacher know, they can then take on the responsibility. **Do not shoulder this burden on your own.**

If you are harming yourself in any way, that is a certain sign that you need some assistance. This may be as simple as finding someone you are able to trust and confide in, or you may require some medical assistance to help you through. **It is most important that you talk with someone!**

'Worry is just fear painting pictures in your mind.'
Jim Rohn

'The best way to cheer yourself up... is to cheer someone else up!'

Mark Twain

'ALL THE STRENGTH YOU NEED TO ACHIEVE ANYTHING IS WITHIN YOU.'
SARA HENDERSON

# Suicide

## . . . help is at hand

As I write this chapter, I hear another story of teenagers taking their lives. The most upsetting thing about the tragic event was that the teens felt they had no other option and no one to talk to about what they were planning to do.

Suicide is final. Once a person succeeds in taking their life, there are no other options. All that is left behind is a string of unanswered questions, guilt and extreme distress for those who loved them.

When I was a teenager, one of my dearest friends decided that suicide was his only option. He was successful in removing himself from the world, but left behind a shattered community of family and friends. My personal anguish and pain regarding the loss of my friend lingered for many years.

You may feel that life is too hard and not worth continuing. But for most people, this is a stage you go through. Yes, it is extremely painful, and there's no denying that. Most people, however, find that they look back on such times and reflect, thankful that they did not take the most extreme and final measure of opting out of life.

If you are feeling suicidal or really wanting to take a ticket out of life, it is so important that you **seek help immediately**. This may be easier said than done. Who do you tell? What if they do not take you seriously?

You can start by telling your parent, school counsellor, teacher or friend. There are also numbers featured at the back of this book that you can call if you need any type of help. The important thing is that you tell someone what you are going through. You are not crazy. You are just going through a tough time like many other people do.

**Look after your body**

**it's the only one**

**you've got!**

# Look after
## yourself

Imagine you have finally purchased your dream car. Shiny at first. A thing of beauty.

You drive it around with pride and visit all your friends. You cannot, however, be bothered washing it, so a mountain of dirt and grease builds up over the first year. You drive and drive the car, but you forget to check the oil and water, not to mention not filling the tank with petrol.

How far do you think you would get? I can tell you now that it would not be long before your prized car would stop. It cannot continue to run without constant attention and good fuel.

Our bodies are a bit like cars. They need constant fuel and care in order to keep them running at their optimum. I read once how we should look after our bodies because they are the only homes we have. We only get one body, so we really need to take the time to care for it.

### diet

Be mindful of your diet. In these days of junk food and processed foods, make sure you try and get at least five portions of fruit and vegetables per day. Likewise, our bodies are made up of more than 50% water. This means that we need to ensure we replace our fluids constantly. Two litres (eight glasses) of water per day is recommended.

Try filling a 1.5 litre plastic bottle with water at the beginning of the day. Carry this bottle around with you and drink from it wherever you go. If this sounds too much, fill a smaller bottle regularly throughout the day. If water is too boring for you, cut a small slice of lemon or lime and pop it in the bottle.

# exercise

## . . . away from the computer screen

Keep your body healthy by making sure you exercise it regularly. In an age when X-Box and DVDs are all the rage, ensure you get out and **MOVE**! Walk to places as often as you can and try to get involved in a regular sport. (No! PlayStation is not a sport!)

Get active to keep the blood pumping around your body.

- Walk the dog
  (or somebody else's)

- Go for a run

- Go for a bike ride with friends

- Take an aerobics class

- Take up a sport, e.g. netball, tennis, football

- Join the local gym

- Rowing or canoeing

- Badminton

- Dancing

- Gymnastics

- Boxing

- Swimming

'Start treating yourself as if you're the most important (asset) you'll ever have. After all, aren't you?'

Anonymous

' Take good care of your body,
It's the only place you have to live.'

Jim Rohn

'The most important words you can say all day are the words you say to yourself, about yourself, when you are alone.'

Chris Helder

**Dealing with parents**

**can be one of the most**

**difficult aspects**

**of being a teenager.**

# parents

**Dealing with parents can be one of the most difficult aspects of being a teenager. Trust me when I say I can speak from experience on this one!**

When you are a teenager, your hormones are out of control, your body is changing and doing weird things. You have a strong desire to gain new independence. And on top of all this, your parents are trying to cope with these changes.

Don't get me wrong here; parents are not perfect, but they are not meant to be. They do not have superhuman strength and knowledge. They are just adults who happen to have a teenager for whom they are responsible. And they are often doing their very best. Now maybe they are doing a lousy job — in your opinion — but just remember, your parents are human.

I was awful to my parents. In fact, I was downright hideous at times. I was not into drugs or alcohol, ever, but I had a poor attitude. And I must admit that I was a fairly selfish person. I treated Mum like a piece of dirt at times (to put it politely) and drove her to tears on many occasions. Why? I honestly don't know. Probably, hormones had a big role to play. Basically, I felt that they had chosen to have me in the first place, so they had better be nice to me and provide everything I wanted!

It wasn't until I had my own children that I realised what an amazing job parents do, and the incredible sacrifices they make just to keep us safe and happy.

Imagine you have bought a new puppy. You love that puppy more than anything. You provide a nice warm bed, food and shelter for your young dog and you worry about it all the time. It stays in the back garden and is fenced in, not

>>>

because you do not trust it, but because you want to ensure its safety and keep it from being attacked or run over. If it gets out of the garden, you worry until you know that it is safe and warm at home again.

Well that is pretty much how your parents feel about you! As a teenager, however, you probably do not resemble a cute little ball of fluff like a puppy. Your parents set up rules and boundaries for you, not to be mean-spirited or awful, but because they have a bit more life experience than you. They know what dangers and temptations are 'out there' in the wider world.

As you get older, your parents will gradually start to loosen those boundaries and you can begin to show them that you will be safe. But remember, your parents are basically acting out of fear much of the time: a fear of you being hurt by others or by your actions. Whatever you believe to be true, your parents truly want the best for you. Try to remember this next time you get angry with them because you cannot go to an all-night party with alcohol and no parents supervising.

**Parents have a bit more life experience than you.**

# SibLing rivalry

Families have their downsides. You may think the real downers are the brothers and sisters your parents put under the same roof.

We can feel like our siblings were created with the prime directive to destroy our day and make life a constant misery. We can also often feel that **we** are blamed for any misunderstandings and fights rather than our siblings, particularly if you are the older child.

I recall many instances when I was blamed for arguments with my younger brother. It seemed to be especially so because I was the older one and 'ought to have known better'!

If you feel constantly taunted or upset by family dynamics, chat with your parents about how you are feeling. (It is best to choose a time when they are calm; not in the middle of a violent screaming match!) Living within a family — particularly with siblings — is just a part of learning to relate to others and will give you life lessons for developing relationships.

Just think about this . . . when you are in the workforce in a few years, you won't get to choose who will work alongside you. Your colleagues will probably be very different from you and may handle conflict in a different way to you. Learning to live in a family environment will prepare you for dealing with many other challenges in life.

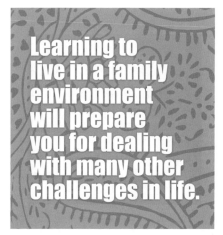

Learning to live in a family environment will prepare you for dealing with many other challenges in life.

# eLdest Child
## syndrome

### . . . it's rough being the eldest!

There is no doubt that being the eldest child can be unfair.

I learnt — being the eldest of two children — that the oldest ones in the family **pave the way** for younger siblings. That means that it is **YOU** who your parents will probably be most strict on! That really seems unfair when it is you who is the subject of most experimentation.

Curfews, bed times, movie choices, parties . . . By the time your younger brothers or sisters enter 'teenage-hood', all the hard work and dramas with parents should be over.

There is no doubt that being a parent of a teenager is also no picnic. Put yourself in a parent's shoes for a minute (just a minute I promise!) and imagine raising a gorgeous, cheeky little monkey such as yourself. Suddenly, your child has become an emotional, independent, crazy teenager who wants vast freedoms to do what he/she wants. For parents, it can be quite difficult to let go a little when a child wants a degree of independence. Many want to hang on to that innocent young child just a bit longer. Who can blame them?

> **Starting off a conversation at a suitable time can mean that both parents and young person can have a level head during their talk.**

So what does that mean for you? You are the eldest child and you want to experience new things and be a bit more independent. Besides, all your other friends can go out whenever they want and go to friend's parties at weekends without parental supervision (or so you think . . .).

You need to look at it first from your parents' point of view. Once you have thought a little about where they are coming from, you can work through some of these issues as they arise.

Talking to your parents at an appropriate time is a good start! Beginning a conversation — during the evening news — about an upcoming party at the weekend is not a good place to start. Try and ask your parents if there is a suitable time you could have a chat with them (perhaps suggest while you wash and dry the dishes together). Starting off a conversation at a suitable time can mean that both parents and young person can have a level head during their talk. Begin by talking to your parents about how responsible you are becoming and how you would like to have a chance to prove that you are trustworthy. If it is a party that you want to attend, discuss this with them, but most importantly **be honest**! There is nothing more lethal to trust than deception. I will repeat this again, **be honest**! If there will be no parents at the party, tell **your** parents. If they then say 'no', try to accept their decision. There will be other opportunities, but be assured, there will probably be very good reasons why they are wary of you attending.   $>>>$

# ELdeSt Child syndrome

I remember being 14 years old, in Year 10 at school.
Being the eldest, I wasn't permitted to do a great deal of
'independent teenager' activities. Practically everyone in my
Year 10 class was invited to a birthday party in a town about
half an hour's train ride from my eastern Melbourne home
suburb. Everyone in my class was allowed to travel by train
on the Friday after school . . . that is, everyone **EXCEPT ME**!

I just could not understand why Mum said 'No'. Everyone
else was allowed to travel on the train together to attend
the party.

We discussed it. Mum wouldn't budge. Either she was going
to drive me to the party (*and pick me up of course!*) or
I would not go!

I agreed. I went and had a great time.

Eventually (when I began my first year at university, aged
17¾), I was allowed to finally travel on the train **all by
myself**!

Another thing that really annoyed me about being the eldest
was that I was always blamed for **everything**, well at
least it seemed like that at the time. Whenever there were
hassles between my younger brother and me, guess who
got the blame. 'You should know better,' I was told. Maybe
I should have known better, but that did not make it the
fault of the eldest child all the time! (*Phew . . . ! Am I glad
I've got that out of my system now!*)

So try to enjoy being the eldest if you possibly can. Just
remember that you will have your licence first and will be
able to go out at weekends **before** your younger siblings.
That will be hard for them to handle. You will be able
to move out of home first and come home to visit your
younger brothers or sisters and quietly annoy them about
parental restrictions.

# intuition

## . . . using your gut instinct

Your intuition can best be described as that little voice inside your head. Sometimes it is a feeling in the pit of your stomach that lets you know the right thing to do.

It is often described as your 'gut instinct'. But how does it work?

Suppose you have an important decision to make. You have been invited to a party next weekend. You know for a fact that a few kids will bring alcohol and no parents will be present.

You know that your parents would definitely not approve of an unsupervised party, yet you would really love to go because many of your friends will be there.

**Take the time to listen to your intuition. It is an important tool.**

Your intuition scans through your enormous database of stored experiences and information, before sending you a signal. For many people, this signal feels a bit like you have got 1,000 butterflies flying around your stomach. For others, it is a feeling of uneasiness. This feeling usually tells us that the party option in question is not the right choice for us.

Alternatively, a situation can arise that poses a different response. You may sense a feeling of being 'at peace' or settled; happy about a decision. This tells you that the decision you are about to make is probably the best one for you.

>>>

125

# intuition

If you are totally stuck and do not know what your intuition is trying to tell you, try this: imagine you have made a definite decision either way about attending that party. Now relax for a moment and believe that you have made that decision. How do you feel? Do you feel at all anxious about attending that party now? If you still feel uneasy, now that you have made your decision, your intuition is probably giving you signals to re-evaluate your decision.

Can you recall a time when you had a 'hunch' about something? It might have been to offer some help to a friend or ring someone. What did you notice? How did you know this was what you needed to do? You probably 'just knew'. This is your intuition at work.

You already possess an amazing ability to 'know' which direction to go. Take the time to listen to your intuition. It is an important tool.

# be careful what you expose yourself to

## Imagine your mind as being like a great big sponge.

Everything you allow into your mind will be absorbed, just as a sponge absorbs liquid. Your mind cannot say, 'No, I choose not to absorb that image!' It does so anyway.

What do you want your mind to absorb?

Think about the programmes you watch on television. What sort of messages are they sending to your mind? You have the power to choose what you are going to allow to influence you, whether that be the movies you watch or the music you listen to.

### movies

You always have a choice to watch certain movies. It is a good idea to make a decision **now** as to what sort of movies you will allow yourself to be exposed to. That way, you can make an easy choice if friends want to see or hire a certain type of movie. I personally choose to never watch a movie beyond a 15 rating. That is a choice I made for myself some time ago because I choose not to have my mind influenced by graphic violence and sexual images.

Do not just go along with the crowd on this one — your mind is a very powerful sponge, so choose wisely.

### television programmes

As with movies, you always have a choice with the TV remote. If the programmes you watch do not meet with your measure of personal integrity — your morals and

>>>

values — change the channel. People often phone television stations to complain about a variety of television shows. However, they always have a simple choice: turn it off or change channels.

It is also important to remember that many television programmes are based on fiction, not real life. The problem with viewing many television programmes is that your mind subconsciously begins to believe that these programmes reflect real life too closely. Programmes like the American *OC* do not reflect what real life is like for the majority of the population, yet our thoughts and reflections may reflect what we think should be a reality. Don't get fooled by this!

## music

Music is a powerful influence; probably one of the most powerful in your life. Choose carefully the music you allow into your mind. It is hard to erase the words and images once they enter your mind. Music, however, can be a really powerfully positive image too. It can help you to relax and feel peaceful. A great thing to do is to look at the lyrics (words) to a song before you buy the album or track. That way you can make a choice whether you want to be influenced by the music and lyrics or not.

## people

We always have a choice as to who we hang out with and allow to influence us. You become like the people you hang out with for most of the time. If you choose to hang out with negative people or troublemakers, chances are you will start to become just like them. If you choose to hang out, however, with positive people and happy people, you will go that way too.

# new communication
# game

## texting, online discussions, email

We live in an amazing time. Communications have come such a long way, even in the past 10 years, and we are now able to communicate with other people instantly.

You have probably heard the line in the *Spiderman* trilogy, that 'with great power comes great responsibility'. That's a good summary of the communication options we have today. With computers, we are now able to have virtually instant conversations with people. We can also join group conversations in chat rooms.

One of the biggest and most alarming problems with these communications is that there is more scope for 'mis-communication', and here begins an entirely new ball game.

> **EXAMPLE: 'I was on Messenger last night and Julie was talking to Kathy about whether I really like John or if I am just stringing him along. I came online and said that I really did like him but I was just annoyed at how he was ignoring me at school. Jack was also online and he was saying that John was going to drop me at school tomorrow.'**

The conversation continues but you get the general idea. A ton of communications occur everyday in what is known as 'cyberspace'. All these instant expressions of feelings and emotions are played out, often in a public arena.

Emails are also very common. In fact, we often find ourselves communicating in written form rather than picking up the telephone, or even better, face to face. Sure it cuts out a lot of time, and you can think carefully about what you >>>

need to say, but one of the biggest issues is that of tone. With email, texting and online discussion sites, you cannot portray the tone you want to express in order to give what you say appropriate context.

### Example: 'Jacqui should get her act together!'

This could be said as a serious statement, or the person may be using sarcasm (a form of joking with people). Jacqui has no way of understanding the tone of that statement because it is not being delivered verbally, with the relevant feelings attached. This is where miscommunication can often occur.

Another issue with this new wave of communication is that many conversations and statements can now be made without the worry of being 'face to face'. With this in mind, we can often say a whole lot that we would not ever feel comfortable saying to someone face to face.

We can now take our time to carefully construct what we want to say, or we may do the opposite and instantly respond to a text without fully thinking through the consequences. The important thing to remember here is that written and typed words are permanent. You cannot rapidly say, 'I didn't mean it!' These forms of instant messaging also do not portray emotion (with the exception of little symbols of happy and sad faces that can be attached to your text!).

There are many cases in which written and typed text messages have been retrieved to deal with crimes or cases of severe bullying.

If you are using computer and mobile communication methods regularly, there are a few useful things that you need to remember in order to protect yourself:

- Take some time to **think through** what you want to say before you send a message or letter. Sometimes we need to put ourselves in the other person's position to better understand how that person may respond.

- If you are feeling hurt or angry about something, simply writing or typing the letter to the other person is enough. You may not need to even send it at all!

- **NEVER, EVER reveal personal details** about yourself.

- Do not give away your phone number or address because you have no way of really ever knowing whether someone else online is pretending to be someone they're not.

- Do not participate in any conversations that you would not normally participate in 'in real life'. If you do not gossip about other people in person, do not do it online. It is exactly the same thing!

- If you do use programs such as Messenger, choose only a small group of contact people, and keep it to that!

- **Be open about what you are doing.** Do not lock yourself away from your family and parents. If you cannot show your parents what you are saying, you may need to rethink what you're saying!

- Before sending an email or text, ask yourself the following simple question, **'Would I be happy saying this in person?'**

# friendships

Most teenagers agree

that their friendships are

probably the most

important part of their lives.

# friendships

## . . . where would we be without friends?

Our relationships with friends can be some of the most special, unique and influential aspects of our lives. Most teenagers agree that their friendships are probably the most important part of their lives. They just would not be able to cope through all the changes and hassles of adolescence without such support.

Have you ever noticed that those people who have the most friends and are constantly surrounded by friends are the friendliest towards others?

As I write this chapter, two of my dear friends have just left after having lunch at my place. We have been friends for 20 years now, which is pretty amazing since we became friends in Year 11. The thing I appreciate about my girlfriends is they have always loved and accepted me for all that I am. If we don't speak to each other for a while, because of the busyness of our lives, it's okay. We know that our friendship is lifelong.

Throughout your teenage years, your friendships will probably chop and change. Some friendships may remain for life, however most won't.

Friendships can be quite seasonal. In primary school, for example, we may have a couple of best friends who we think will be our very best friends forever. Then we may move on and go to separate secondary schools and lose touch with these friends. We then make new sets of friends in secondary school, then university or work and so on.

Friendships are an absolute God-given gift. They can be unique and special and certainly help us get through the happy and the difficult seasons of our lives. Real friends are different from the variety of people you will meet

>>>

throughout your life and be friendly with (acquaintances). Real friendships are built on honesty and a solid relationship of trust. They stand the test of time.

Interestingly enough, you may only have a small handful of truly good friends throughout your life. Two of my dearest friends are from my latter school years (now 20-year friendships), whilst most recent friendships have developed in my working life and through relationships I have developed with other mums. Another important friendship is from my teen years. That relationship has stood the test of time as we have experienced joys and tragedies together.

It is true that if you want great friendships, you have to first be a good friend. And if you want more friends, be one to others.

**If you want great friendships, you have to first be a good friend.**

# comfort
# levels

*A true friend should never pressure you into doing something that makes you feel uncomfortable.*

A number of years ago, in my late teens, a friend of mine was having a group of friends over one night.

He attended a different school to me but we had forged a friendship because we lived close to each other. He and his friends attended a high-profile private school.

That evening, the group proceeded to light up a 'bong' containing marijuana. It was a drug I had never seen before. To be honest, I had made the choice to put my health first and to stay clear of drugs.

That night, I was offered a smoke of marijuana.

'No thanks,' I replied.

'Are you sure?' he asked.

'Yep, absolutely,' I replied.

And that was that! There was no pressure, no snide remark about being a 'wuss', and I felt completely at ease.

I realised that night that my friend valued our friendship beyond keeping in with his friends and doing drugs.

> A true friend should never pressure you into doing something that makes you feel uncomfortable.

**NO BODY**

**IS PERFECT!**

# body image
## no body's perfect

If you only get one thing from reading this book, it is this: absolutely, totally, unequivocally, NO BODY IS PERFECT IN THE WHOLE UNIVERSE. Just in case you didn't get that, I will repeat it again . . . **NO BODY IS PERFECT**!

It has taken me a long time to understand and acknowledge this, but if you can grab hold of this truth now, it might just save you a few years of heartache and wasted time spent trying to achieve something that is quite simply unachievable.

In the society in which we live, we are constantly bombarded with body images that we just cannot live up to. In almost every magazine we pick up, we are faced with numerous body images of people that are neither true nor realistic.

> **We are constantly bombarded on a daily basis with body images that we just cannot live up to.**

Did you realise that when you see a picture of a young model or actor in a magazine that they have spent anywhere up to four hours being primped and preened by up to a dozen stylists? They do not simply turn up to the photographic studio and begin the photo shoot. They have to arrive up to four hours before so that a team of hairdressers, make-up artists, dressers and stylists can ensure that they look 'perfect' for the photo shoot. Finally, once the chosen photos reach the magazine layout department, a team of professionals work at 'cleaning up' the image using computer enhancements. This can include anything from removing spots or blemishes, taking away shadows under the eyes, whitening teeth and the whites of

> > >

the eyes, even 'shaving off' inches from legs and bottoms. This is known in the industry as 'airbrushing'. Do you actually realise the lengths that these magazines go to so they can make you see these images and portray them as normal?

Having worked in the television industry on a part-time basis whilst studying at university, I have experienced first hand the amount of work that goes into preparing a person for the television screen. When an actor arrives on the set to begin a day of filming, they are usually very unglamorous and hardly recognisable as the person you see on your television screens. Some people have literally just got out of bed, thrown on some clothes and jumped in the car for work. Once again, it is left to a team of professionals to work their magic. A team of staff will ensure the actor's hair is just perfect, their outfit is organised, ironed and fits perfectly, and make-up is gleamingly 'natural'. No wonder people often comment that an actor or television personality 'looks very different' when encountered in the street or at a venue.

Take, for example, glamour photography. It is quite amazing when you see the transformation, and it often hardly looks like the actual person at all. It is so important you remember that the majority of images you are faced with on a daily basis — whether it be in magazines or on TV — are images that have been made by a team of professionals! You cannot possibly live up to these images unless you have a professional team of stylists who can work with you every single day. (Believe me, there are some actors and entertainers who can afford to have a team like this, and do!)

'You can always tell
a real friend:

When you've made
a fool of yourself
he doesn't make you feel
you've done
a permanent job!'

Lawrence J. Peter
Canadian Writer

'The only
way to have
a friend is
to be one.'
Ralph Waldo
Emerson

'Friendship
with oneself
is all important
because without it
one cannot be
friends with
anyone else
in the world.'
Eleanor Roosevelt

'My best friend is the one who
brings out the best in me.'
**Henry Ford**

It is amazing that

small comments can have

such an impact on body image.

# i hate my body!

## Whether we like it or not, we all have to accept the bodies we have.

Sure, we can go under the knife and have our bodies altered in various ways. But realistically, most of us do not have the money or the endurance to go through countless operations to achieve what society and the media tell us is the perfect body. And do you want to know something else? You could go through all the operations in the world and still not feel good about your body at the end of it all. This is because our bodies will never be perfect, and they will constantly change with diet, exercise and age, no matter what!

I was a scrawny teenager, and had legs like bean poles even though I was short. But I always had a thing about my butt. I was always petrified that it would grow into this huge monstrous organ with its own mind and personality. I remember, one time when I was in Year 8 (aged 13), my brother made an unkind remark about my bottom. His exact words for my butt were 'Lard-ass' and 'Boomer Butt'. Now I bet you can imagine how paranoid those comments made me feel. Though nothing could have been further from the truth, in typical brother style, he said whatever he knew would get a reaction from me. The problem was, it planted a thought in my mind that would repeat itself again and again and again. I began to watch everything that I ate, and for a time, I only ate apples for breakfast, lunch and dinner if I could get away with it.

**You could go through all the operations in the world and still not feel good about your body at the end of it all.**

>>>

143

# i hate my body!

It is amazing that small comments can have such an impact on body image. Ironically, now some 20 years later, my brother's daughter and I both now wear the same sized clothing and he teases me now about having a little girl's skinny body. Brothers!

There is not a lot you can do about your basic body type. It is all in the genetics you inherited. Most of us will have a body quite similar to our mother's or father's. In my case, I have a body very similar to my mum's. I am short in stature and tend to carry fat in the same areas that she does. You have the body that you have been given and you need to make the choice to be happy with what you have, sooner or later (better to be sooner!).

Even the most gorgeous models in the world can have body image issues. They still think their butts are big or their boobs are too small. No one is exempt from these feelings.

**Even the most gorgeous models in the world can have body image issues.**

eight//

# bULLying

**Unfortunately some people
choose to bully others to
make themselves feel bigger.**

# dealing with
# bULLYing

When most of us think of bullying, we immediately think of being backed into a corner of a classroom when the teacher is out of the room; being either verbally threatened or actually physically assaulted.

I remember as a Year 7 student, new to my secondary school, being locked in the storeroom cupboard of the classroom by a tall fellow student. That was just because I was the new girl and she didn't really like me.

But in fact, whilst physical bullying does still unfortunately occur, it is the emotional type of bullying that can be just as hurtful and can stay with young people well into their adult lives and beyond.

## examples of bullying

- Physically hitting, punching or shoving another person, intentionally.

- Name calling.

- Deliberately provoking someone, making fun of them.

- Making someone to do something they do not want to do.

- Excluding someone from your activities.

- Gossiping.

- Writing hurtful or nasty emails, letters or text messages.

'I didn't belong as a kid
and that always bothered me.
If only I'd known that one day
my differences would be an asset,
then my early life would have
been much easier.'

Bette Midler

'If you want people
to be glad to meet you,
you must first be
glad to meet them,
and show it.'

Johann von Goethe

'Do not be afraid of enthusiasm

You need it

You can do nothing effectively
without it.'

Francois Pierre Guillaume Guizot

# a bullying
# example

I saw a woman on an American talk show — then in her late 30s — complaining that she could not move forward in her life. She explained how she had suffered immense emotional and verbal bullying 20 years before.

The culprit had been a fellow female student at her school. The victim had become pregnant as a teenager and suffered a great deal of verbal abuse from other girls and one 'popular and attractive' girl in particular. Both women were reunited on the show in front of a studio audience.

The victim was still, to that day, absolutely devastated by the childhood bullying.

She had carried around a burden of rejection and hurt for two decades.

The most frightening thing was the reaction of the alleged bully. She claimed she had no recollection of the girl or of the verbal attacks she had made.

She apologised but remained incredulous at the degree of hurt she had caused.

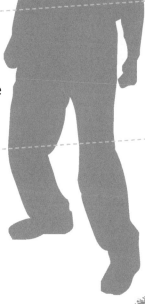

'Sticks and stones may break my
bones but words will never harm me.'

# Sticks and stones

## . . . name-calling is bullying

You know the saying, 'Sticks and stones may break my bones but words will never harm me'? What a load of garbage!

I can vividly recall verbal bullying, way back as a 12-year-old, in Year 7. I have always been someone of small stature, and was easily the smallest in my class back then. One fellow student came up with the nickname 'Weasel' for me. I absolutely hated that. It made me feel like some awful little animal. Why couldn't they think up a title like 'Little Cutie' or something like that?

Well, I coped pretty well until the last day of the school year when our class teacher was giving out Christmas cards. They were lovely hand-made cards with a caricature of each of us on the front. As mine came around, I couldn't believe my eyes; right there above my very cute portrait was the word 'Weasel'! I couldn't believe that even my teacher had picked up on that name!

Well, I am still small in stature, but I don't let it bother me.

I tell this story to illustrate, though, that names 'stick'! Some 25 years later, I can still recall that experience as though it was yesterday.

*'Kind words heal and help; cutting words wound and maim.'*

*Proverbs 15:4*

**Your tongue**

**can be like a sword . . .**

# your tongue,
# a sword?

You may be a person who occasionally calls people names, for whatever reason. You need to understand that the words that come out of your mouth can have a lasting effect on someone, though you may not think so at the time. You may say, 'Oh, but they know that I am only joking.' Well they may **say** that, but words have a way of sticking in our minds if they are offensive or hurtful. And they can replay themselves over and over again like a recording in our minds for as long as we allow them to. So please, remember that your tongue is a very powerful weapon, even though you may not physically hurt someone . . . you may cause even greater emotional damage.

You need to make sure that the words that come out of your mouth will not cause someone else to feel bad. Use your words to build others up, not destroy their self-image.

## People keep bullying me!

So, what if you are currently at the mercy of a bully?

The usual advice is to 'just ignore' the bully. But that is easier said than done. The most important thing for you to remember is that you are unique and valued! Your value is not in what others think of you or say about you. The most important thing is that you believe that you are amazing and valuable. You also need to know that the people that bully others usually do so for a reason. They may have a lot of difficult issues of self-worth of their own. The main reason why people bully others is

> **Use your words to build others up, not destroy their self-image.**

> > >

that they see elements of value in others that they wish they had. So they try to wear their victim down.

Also, remember that people can only put you down as far as you will allow them to. If you choose to ignore them and only listen to the positive words people speak to you, then you retain the power.

So try it! Next time someone says something negative to you, repeat a positive affirmation (positive word or phrase) to yourself internally. You could say something to yourself like, 'I know that I am worthwhile and important', or 'I am beautiful and lovely'. You should feel much better.

It is also important to remember that if you cannot say something positive to someone, don't say anything at all.

*'When you're kind to others, you help yourself; when you're cruel to others, you hurt yourself.'*

*Proverbs 11:17*

**If you cannot say something positive to someone, don't say anything at all.**

'Human character is formed not in the absence of difficulty but in our response to the difficulty.'

Jim Rohn

'Start treating yourself as if you're the most important asset you'll ever have.

After all, aren't you?'

Anonymous

'Some of the best lessons we ever learn, we learn from our mistakes and our failures. The error of the past is the success and wisdom of the future.'

Tyron Edwards

quotes

**Ignoring someone**

**takes away all their**

**bully power and it**

**all comes back to you!**

# bULLy bUSterS

## ignore your bully

Bullies actually get their power from you, only if you give it away. Every time you react, you give the bully the result they were after. Ignoring someone takes away all their bully power and it all comes back to you!

## say 'NO!'

As soon as you say this single, powerful word, you are letting the bully know loud and clear that what they are doing or saying is not okay. If you struggle a bit with this at first, start by saying it under your breath or in your mind until you have the courage to say it out loud and with authority. You are worth it! Saying 'No' loud and clear also lets everyone else around you know that what is happening is not okay. They are a witness to what is happening and your desire for it not to happen again!

## get help

If you are at school, it is really important that you let a teacher know as soon as you are the victim of a bully. Most schools have in place (or should do) very strict anti-bullying policies. If you cannot talk to your teacher, ask a friend to go on your behalf or to go with you.

Talk to your parents. They will deal with this on your behalf, and can talk to your teacher or head teacher. >>>

**A bully is really just someone who is lacking confidence in his or her self.**

# bULLY bUSteRs

If you are in the workplace, bullying of any kind should also be against the rules. Tell your boss what is happening to you; they must act on this information. There have been many reported cases of severe injury due to workplace pranks or bullying, so never put up with it. You are worth way more than that!

## stand tall and have confidence

Bullies are looking for someone from whom they can steal confidence. Try and remember that a bully is really just someone who is lacking confidence in his or her self. A bully tries to make others feel inferior to hide their own insecurities. When you remember this, you realise the bully is just a person who lacks confidence.

## don't look the other way if you see someone being bullied

If you see a friend or someone else being bullied, you owe it to them to let someone know, or step in for them. Make sure you do not get involved with a situation of physical bullying; instead, call for assistance. Looking the other way and ignoring a bullying situation is just as bad as being the bully yourself.

**Looking the other way and ignoring a bullying situation is just as bad as being the bully yourself.**

# positive **defence**

**When someone is bullying you, it is usually because that person feels pretty awful about themselves in some way.**

Often people pick on those parts of you that they may feel bad about in themselves, e.g. they might say, 'You're fat and ugly.' What they are really saying is that they do not like things about their own body.

Try and say some positive things to the person bullying you.

That is a difficult 'ask', I know, but just watch the bully's confidence grow as you begin to make positive deposits into their self-esteem account!

# making positive Life choices

# Choose
## your influences

If you hang around negative people all the time, the chances are fairly high that you will soon become a pretty negative person. Other people's attitudes and opinions can have a huge impact on us.

> The people we choose to spend our time with have a great influence – both positive or negative – on us.

Have you ever been put in a group to work on a class assignment only to find that the teacher has put you with two extremely unmotivated people? Often in such a situation the motivated student is dragged down by the rest of the group's negativity and lack of focus. Then notice the difference in a group's productivity if you put two motivated students with a fairly negative and unmotivated person. The positive students will quite often motivate the team to achieve its collective best and complete an amazing assignment.

The people we choose to spend our time with have a great influence — positive or negative — on us. What sort of people do you choose to hang out with?

**Example:** A teenage girl began hanging around with a negative crowd. They were part of a local gang whose members hung out at the local railway station, harassing others, smoking and using foul language. Most of these teens lived in government-funded housing for troubled youth. They told the girl of all their freedoms, being able to stay out late with few rules. To someone who knew no different, this seemed like a great life. It seemed they could do everything that her parents prevented her from doing. They had very few boundaries and no parents breathing down their necks.

This girl soon began allowing negative influences to change her attitudes, and the way she spoke to her parents and teachers.

If you hang around the wrong people for too long, you soon will become just like the people that your parents warn you against. If you choose to spend your time with a person who does not care about school or achieving good results, soon you will not care much either.

Make a choice, instead, to spend your time with people who have a positive influence on your life and your self-image. Spend time with friends who build you up rather than tear you and others down.

**They are called drugs**

**because they are addictive.**

# smoking and **drugs**

One of the most common sayings I used to hear as a teenager was, 'If Sarah told you to jump off a cliff, would you do that too?'

The best advice concerning any type of drug is to not try them. You may, however, be reading this book now and it is too late. You may have tried smoking. I think that it is fairly normal to be inquisitive about things like smoking. We wonder what it is like. The important thing to remember, however, is that they are called drugs because they are addictive. This means that from the first time you smoke, your body can become hooked on a certain drug you smoke, whether it be tobacco or a stronger substance such as marijuana. The problem with drugs is that our body begins to develop a tolerance for them and the need becomes greater for something stronger or more often. You can be extremely lucky and never get hooked, but who wants to take the chance?

With all the media attention these days concerning the harmful affects of smoking, I do not understand why anyone would willingly take up smoking. Who really wants to have black, tar-infested lungs, and sticky fat stuck to the inside of their arteries? The ads on television are enough to make you feel ill anyway, without having to risk developing life-threatening diseases.

# in CONCLUSION . . .

## . . . where to from here?

This is not the end! You have reached the last pages of this book but, hopefully, you are set to take hold of every opportunity heading your way. I hope that you have also gained a bit of helpful advice along the way.

I urge you to revisit the chapters regularly and see them as guideposts along the way to being a passionate and amazing person, well beyond your teenage years.

You need to remember always that you are an amazing person with an abundance of potential. Maybe you had not quite realised that just yet, but hopefully you do now.

You live in an amazing world that is just bursting to give you all the opportunities and experiences that you desire, well beyond your past and present circumstances. It is what is inside you that is amazing.

**Go on, give it all you've got!**

*Shaz*

# helpful teen
# Support lines and websites

**Childline** — emotional support for children and young people on issues relating to child abuse, bullying, etc.
0800 1111 *www.childline.org.uk*

**Teen Challenge** — help conquering addictions
01269 844168  *www.teenchallenge.org.uk*

**Beat (Eating Disorders Association) for young people** — help with eating disorders
0845 634 7650 *www.b-eat.co.uk/YoungPeople*

**Self-harm** — if you are self-harming or know someone who is
*www.selfharm.co.uk*

**Young Minds** — mental health and emotional wellbeing
*www.youngminds.org.uk*

**Samaritans** — talk to someone
UK: 08457 90 90 90    ROI: 1850 60 90 90
*www.samaritans.org*

**Brook Young People's Information Service** — teenage pregnancy and sexual health
0808 802 1234  *www.brook.org.uk*

**Eighteen and Under** — support and information for anyone under 18 who has suffered sexual, physical or emotional abuse
0800 731 40 8 *www.18u.org.uk*

**Talk Don't Walk** — support and advice for young people who have run away from home or are thinking of running away from home or care
0800 085 2136

**Kids Health** — dealing with issues like body image, sexual health, drugs, alcohol etc  *www.kidshealth.org/teen*

**Teenage Health Freak** — lots of information including advice and information on bullying, eating disorders, legal rights, self harm, suicidal, confidentiality when seeing a GP
*www.teenagehealthfreak.net*

**Parentlineplus** — support for parents
0808 800 2222 *www.gotateenager.org.uk*

# about the author

**Sharon Witt** is a bestselling author and speaker whose passion is to equip and empower today's youth to live amazing and impacting lives.

Her popular teen books include
**Teen Talk, Teen Talk — Girl Talk, Teen Talk — Guy Talk.**

Sharon has been a High School teacher for more than eighteen years. She lives in Melbourne, Australia with her very supportive husband Andrew, and children Josh and Emily.

## www.teentalkinternational.com

# notes